EMOTIONAL INTELLIGENCE AND PROJECTS

Nicholas Clarke, PhD, Ranse Howell

Emotional Intelligence and Projects

ISBN: 978-1-933890-98-2

Published by: Project Management Institute, Inc.
14 Campus Boulevard
Newtown Square, Pennsylvania 19073-3299 USA.
Phone: +610-356-4600
Fax: +610-356-4647
E-mail: customercare@pmi.org
Internet: www.PMI.org

Acknowledgments

The authors would like to thank the University of Southampton, UK and the Centre for Effective Dispute Resolution, London, UK, and those project managers who agreed to participate in this research and who remained committed to the pilot research project throughout. With special thanks to Norinne Betjemann, Scott Stapleton, Michael Saunders, Paul Bates, Joanne Grant, and the members of the UK Chapter of PMI for their assistance and support. We would also like to acknowledge gratitude to Isabel Phillips and Tracey Commock from CEDR for their assistance in delivering parts of the EI training.

Thanks also to the Project Management Institute for funding the research and Professor Terry Williams at the University of Southampton for acting as liaison on the Research Project. Any opinions, findings, conclusions, or recommendations expressed in this research are those of the authors and do not necessarily reflect the view of the Project Management Institute.

The Authors

This book is a collaborative reseach project between academics at the University of Southampton (UoS) School of Management and staff at the Centre for Effective Dispute Resolution (CEDR), a not-for-profit organization based in London that is recognized internationally for its work in conflict resolution and mediation. CEDR played a significant role in designing and delivering part of the EI training program. The research team comprised Dr. Nicholas Clarke from the University of Southampton School of Management, and Ranse Howell, Projects Manager at CEDR.

CONTENTS

SECTION 1.0

Summary of the Report

How to successfully participate and manage projects in order that projects meet their desired outcomes has become more significant over recent years, as project working has become a preferred and dominant form of work organization within an environment of increasing complexity (Sicotte & Langley, 2000; Olson, Walker, Rueckert, & Bonner, 2001). Key dimensions of projects considered to be associated with successful outcomes have been both appropriate collaborative behaviors on behalf of project members as well as transformational leadership. More recently, emotional intelligence (EI) (Brackett, Mayer & Warner, 2004; Mayer, Roberts, & Barsade, 2008) has been suggested as a unique area of individual differences that is likely to underpin the required behaviors associated with these project activities (Druskat & Druskat, 2006), although to date actual research evidence examining EI in projects is minimal (c.f. Leban & Zulauf, 2004; Muller & Turner, 2007).

To date only five studies have appeared in the literature specifically investigating emotional intelligence in project contexts, all of which have examined relationships between emotional intelligence and either leadership or project management competences. Together these studies suggest a significant role for emotional intelligence in terms of underpinning both leadership and important behaviors that have been suggested as associated with successful outcomes in projects. However, these EI and project studies do suffer a number of major limitations. The first of these relates to criticisms associated with the validity of the particular EI measures used. Another limitation is that no attempt was made to control for both general ability or personality.

Given the limitations with some of the previous studies examining emotional intelligence in projects, this research study seeks to build on the current literature in two major ways. Firstly, through investigating whether emotional intelligence is associated with a number of behaviors posited as key for successfully working in project contexts. Secondly, through using an ability-based model of emotional intelligence and controlling for both cognitive ability and personality, the extent to which emotional intelligence is able to account for variance in these behaviors over and above these other variables, can be more clearly determined. From a project management perspective there is also a need for studies that examine EI development interventions and whether these can be tracked to improvements in the attitudes and behaviors necessary for project management. Despite significant interest in the concept of emotional intelligence within project management (Druskat & Druskat, 2006), this is still a relatively unexplored concept within the field. Although some progress has been made in examining relationships between emotional intelligence and project management behaviors associated with leadership (Muller & Turner, 2007), research examining interventions for developing emotional intelligence in project managers is very much embryonic. The findings from the one evaluation study so far conducted by Turner and Lloyd-Walker (2008), although using a competence-based measure of emotional intelligence, also suggest that designing training interventions that are targeted specifically for project management may be an important factor to consider in maximizing the effectiveness of any training. This pilot research therefore sought to address the following objectives:

1. To identify the relationships between emotional intelligence abilities and specific project manager competences identified as critical within project contexts.
2. To identify relationships between emotional intelligence and transformational leadership behaviors.
3. To determine whether training can result in improvements in project managers' emotional intelligence abilities and relevant project management competences.
4. To identify factors that may be associated with the effectiveness of emotional intelligence training.

Based on a sample of 67 UK project managers, it was found that emotional intelligence ability measures and empathy explained additional variance in the project manager competences of teamwork, attentiveness, and managing conflict, and the transformational leadership behaviors of idealized influence and individualized consideration after controlling for cognitive ability and personality. In addition, a 6-month follow-up of 53 project managers who attended a 2-day emotional intelligence training program found statistically significant changes in the emotional intelligence ability, understanding emotions. The results support a growing body of literature that suggest emotional intelligence, when perceived as a distinct set of independent cognitive-emotional abilities, may indeed be an important aspect of individual difference that can help to explain the performance of project managers in key areas associated with relationship management in projects. Further, the results suggest that such abilities may in fact be developed and improved through training and development interventions.

SECTION 2.0

Emotions, Emotional Intelligence, and Projects

2.1 Critical Perspectives on Project Management: Projects are Emotional

Traditionally, research in the area of project management has tended to direct its attention to the application of tools and techniques with far less attention given to the role of people management and the management of relationships more specifically (Cooke-Davis, 2002; Matta & Ashkenas, 2003; Munns & Bjeirmi, 1996; Verma, 1996). Over the past two decades however, the "human side" of project management has increasingly been identified as a critical component of the project manager's role and associated with project management success (Cleland, 1995; Cooke-Davies, 2002; Cowie, 2003; El-Sabaa, 2001; Hill, 1977; Kliem & Ludin, 1992; Lechler, 1998; Sizemore, 1988). Given that project management involves attempting to get the best input from a wide range of technical specialists, many authors have identified a large part of the project manager's role in particular as one that constitutes leadership and relationship management between all the parties involved in a project (Milosevic, Inman & Ozbay, 2001; Sizemore 1988; Strohmeier, 1992). Baker, Murphy, & Fisher (1983) showed that of the seven factors they identified, which together accounted for 91% of the variance between projects that succeeded and those that failed, one factor, coordination and relations, accounted on its own for 77% of the variance perceived in project success. This included areas such as the project manager's human skills and characteristics associated with the project team itself, including project team spirit, participation in decision-making, a sense of mission, and supportive informal relations between team members. Similarly, more recently Rudolf, Wagner, & Fawcett (2008) also have found the behavioral dimension of project management, which included communication, involvement, motivation, and identifying conflicts, contributes to greater project success in addition to other structural and procedural factors (Milosevic, et al 2001). Until very recently, however, this focus on factors associated with managing relationships was seen from a primarily administrative and functionalist perspective, the underlying assumption being that if its importance to project work was emphasized sufficiently enough, and a set of project work practices associated with it were codified, then this key aspect of a project's effectiveness could be sufficiently organized, planned, and of course controlled (Kerzner, 2001; Dvir, Raz, & Shenhar, 2003). As a result, relatively few studies have examined how relationships and their management are enacted within project contexts or how the patterns and dynamics of these relationships come to exert key influences within projects (Grundy, 2000; Webb, 2000). Partly in response to reports that the results of projects often fail to meet the expectations of their stakeholders (O'Connor & Reinsborough, 1992), alongside a growing recognition of the limitations of traditional approaches for analyzing the problems and challenges encountered in the project management field, a range of alternative and more pluralist approaches to examine these behavioral and relationship dimensions have been called for (Cicmil & Hodgson, 2006; Kreiner, 1995; Packendorff, 1995; Winter, Smith, Morris, & Cicmil, 2006; Williams, 1999). For many writers, this represents a need to reorientate far more research to understand the "actuality" of projects, in order to better understand the real, lived experience of project management that might then help build more effective bridges from research to practice (Cicmil, Williams, Thomas, & Hodgson, 2006). An important focus is the recognition that projects can themselves be seen as constituting a social process, and that we can learn more about how different areas of project management contribute to project success if we begin to analyze how the relationships through which project management takes place are defined and redefined, negotiated, and enacted. To date, such an approach has provided new insights into the nature of relationships in project management and their influence on outcomes, particularly through, for example, understanding the roles that power and politics play as collaboration to achieve project objectives becomes subject to divergent interests or understandings (Cicmil & Marshall, 2005; O'Leary & Williams, 2008; Pinto, 2000). Similarly, our understanding of why and how problems occur in projects and how, and if they are dealt with, has increased through seeking to identify the nature of learning processes in projects, how these develop, and the factors which may impede or support learning (Keegan & Turner, 2001; Phang, Kankanhalli, & Ang, 2008; Sense, 2003).

A major area which has received minimal attention within the project management field has been the recognition of the role that emotions play within projects. In recognizing projects as social processes, this suggests that projects are, in their very nature, major sources of emotion. The social interactions through which relationships in projects are constructed and developed are inherently emotional, and it follows then that emotions are likely to play a significant role in influencing both their development and trajectory within a project setting (Weiss & Cropanzano, 1996). The fact that patterns of social interactions in groups are associated with group outcomes has been recognized for some time now (Steiner, 1972; Weick & Roberts, 1993). To date, however, very little research has been conducted that has sought to understand how emotions are generated in projects, how these are managed, and importantly how they affect both behaviors and decisions that then impact on project outcomes. This itself is somewhat of an anomaly given the wealth of literature that has identified the significance of conflict in projects (Chen, 2006; Porter & Lilly, 1996; Tarr, 2007) and recognizing that conflict is a source of major emotion (Barki & Hartwick, 2004; Bodtker & Jameson, 2001).

Although research-examining emotions within organizations more generally have long been neglected (Muchinsky 2000), over more recent years, there has been an increasing amount of research demonstrating how emotions are implicated in key work behaviors and processes that have considerable implications for project management. For example, emotions have been found to play a major role in framing task-directed processes, such as effort and cooperation within teams and groups (Pirola-Merlo, Hartel, Mann, & Hirst, 2002; Sy, Cote, & Saavedra, 2005). A number of studies have also shown how the emotional states of employees influence their performance. Positive affect, in particular, has been found to contribute to managerial performance (Staw & Barsade, 1993), group motivation, and coordination (Barsade, 2002; Sy, Cote, & Saavedra, 2005), creativity (Amabile, Barsade, Mueller, & Staw, 2005), cognitive flexibility (Isen & Daubman, 1984), and pro-social behaviors (George & Brief, 1992). Organizational research into emotions within work contexts has also identified the major role they play in shaping attitudes, actions, and decision-making (Weiss & Cropanzano, 1996). Trust and commitment considered so important to the effectiveness of projects, for example, are recognized as possessing major emotional dimensions (Erdem & Ozen, 2003; McAllister, 1995; Meyer, Stanley, Herscovitch, & Topolntsky, 2002). Similarly, the role of project managers, in articulating a clear vision for project success and inspiring the project team, is seen as engendering an emotional attachment (Druskat & Druskat, 2006; George, 2000). To date, however, very little empirical research has examined emotions in projects and their impact on processes and outcomes. Recently, Peslak (2005) recorded the emotional states of 55 students from 18 teams involved on a team project over 15 weeks and showed how individuals on these projects experienced a variety of emotions over the project's lifetime. He found that these teams began their projects in a lower emotional state but their level of emotional involvement increased throughout the life of the project, with increases found in emotional intensity. Importantly, the final emotions were significant factors in team process satisfaction. This suggests that there may well be significant differences in both project member behaviors and project outcomes, depending upon how well project managers are able to recognize, understand, and manage the emotional content arising from project work. Individual abilities or competences such as these have been referred to in the literature as comprising emotional intelligence, and a number of authors have suggested that such abilities may differentiate more effective project managers (Butler & Chinowsky, 2006; Leban & Zulauf, 2004; Muller & Turner, 2007). This is based on research that has begun to identify significant relationships between emotional intelligence and team effectiveness (e.g., Feyerherm & Rice, 2002; Jordan & Troth, 2004), leadership (e.g., Barling, Slater, & Kelloway, 2000; Rosete & Ciarrochi, 2005) as well as research specifically within projects (e.g., Leban & Zulauf, 2004; Muller & Turner, 2007).

2.2 The Concept of Emotional Intelligence

The concept of emotional intelligence first came to the attention of many organizations and managers when Daniel Goleman published his first book of the same name, which was followed by a second book some 3 years later (Goleman, 1995, 1998). The first scientific paper on the topic was published somewhat earlier in 1990 by Peter Salovey and John Mayer (Salovey & Mayer, 1990). The concept itself, however, has much earlier roots that can be traced back to some of the pioneering work into behavior by Edward Thorndike in the 1920s. Thorndike is credited with recognizing that intelligence may include a wide range of intelligence domains and identified social intelligence as a separate set of interpersonal-related abilities considered to comprise a form of intelligence. He originally defined social intelligence as "the ability to understand and manage men and women, boys and girls—to act wisely in human relations" (Thorndike, 1920). Later, problems with developing valid measures for accurately assessing social intelligence was a key reason for its becoming increasingly marginalized within research on human intelligence such that it became omitted from most traditional perspectives of intelligence (Thurstone, 1938; Spearman, 1927; Wecshler, 1958). It has not been until more recently that the notion of social and affective dimensions of intelligence has again begun to receive attention. Most notably, initially with the publication of work by Howard Gardner, who proposed the existence of seven intelligence domains of which social intelligence, comprising a person's intrapersonal and interpersonal intelligence was one. Although extending beyond just emotional content, both of these domains placed significance emphasis on abilities associated with recognizing sets of feelings in oneself and distinguishing the feelings and moods of others as key aspects of social intelligence (Gardner, 1983). Salovey and Mayer's (1990) initial paper on emotional intelligence identified it as a subset of social intelligence and characterized the concept as consisting of a set of four interrelated cognitive abilities associated with the processing of emotional information. Similar to the notion of intelligence more widely, it describes the ability to reason about a particular type of information. They define it as follows:

> "the ability to perceive accurately, appraise, and express emotion; the ability to access and/or generate feelings when they facilitate thought; the ability to understand emotion and emotional knowledge; and the ability to regulate emotions to promote emotional and intellectual growth" (Mayer & Salovey, 1997, p. 10).

However, throughout the 1990s a number of differing conceptualizations of emotional intelligence or models have been proposed, igniting considerable debate as to the theoretical validity of the concept (Conte, 2005; Locke, 2005). Although there is some degree of overlap between many of these models (for example, most include an emphasis on emotional awareness), essentially they differ quite markedly in how they perceive the EI construct, how it is measured, and the relationships which the construct potentially has to other relevant aspects of human functioning. Generally these differing models can be categorized as either ability-based conceptualizations of EI, mixed-model, conceptualizations, and competence-based approaches, although some models do not always fit neatly into either grouping. Some of the most widely used models in the literature and their features are as follows:

2.2.1 Ability Models of Emotional Intelligence

The ability model of emotional intelligence (Salovey & Mayer, 1990; Mayer & Salovey, 1997; Mayer, Roberts, & Barsade, 2008) is widely regarded as the most scientifically robust model of emotional intelligence in that it meets the criteria far more closely than others for what is termed an independent intelligence. The four abilities are cognitive in nature and are argued as developing from early childhood onwards. These four abilities are considered to develop and are therefore arranged in a hierarchical fashion in the following order: (1) ability to perceive emotion; (2) ability to integrate emotion to facilitate thought; (3) ability to understand emotions; and (4) ability to manage emotions. These are measured in a similar fashion to other intelligence tests through assessing a person's knowledge; in this instance the assessment is made on eight individual tasks, two relating to each ability or branch on a test called the MSCEIT (Mayer-Salovey-Caruso Emotional Intelligence Test, Mayer, Salovey, & Caruso, 2002). Over the past 15 years, there has been considerable work undertaken in developing the metric and establishing its validity, with promising results. For example, it correlates only modestly with other forms of cognitive ability (e.g., verbal and perceptual reasoning [Mayer, Roberts, & Barsade, 2008], and aspects of personality such as openness and agreeableness [Day & Carroll, 2004; Lopes, Salovey, & Strauss, 2003]), thereby offering some support for the independent nature of the construct. Criterion-related tests involving studies that investigate how the ability model relates or predicts life outcomes or behaviors have also been theoretically consistent with the nature of the construct within a range of differing domains. Some of the more important outcomes have included findings that show their relationship with aspects of social functioning (Brackett et al., 2006; Lopes et al., 2004), psychological well-being (Brackett & Mayer, 2003; Brackett et al., 2006), and a number of important work-related outcomes, including decision making and negotiation (Day & Carroll, 2004; Mueller & Curhan, 2007).

The ability model of EI has also been the driver for and underpins a number of other EI models and measures. These models converge with some consensus for accepting the theoretical validity of the four branch or ability structure as comprising emotional intelligence but have developed alternative approaches for considering how it is best to be measured. Schutte et al. (1998) developed a 33-item scale, which differs in that it attempts to assess an individual's emotional intelligence through the use of a self-report questionnaire. The obvious advantage here is the much reduced cost and resources involved in administering the test. Jordan, Ashkanasy, Hartel, and Hooper (2002), by contrast, developed a measure of emotional intelligence designed to specifically assess the emotional intelligence within teams rather than individuals called the Workgroup Emotional Intelligence Profile (WEIP). This relies on team members rating each other on a number of EI dimensions corresponding to these four EI abilities as well as providing self assessments.

2.2.2 Mixed Models of Emotional Intelligence

Mixed models of emotional intelligence are so called due to the inclusion of a range of noncognitive capabilities or personality traits as part of their overall conceptualization of the construct. As a result, many of the measures used to assess emotional intelligence from this perspective have received some degree of criticism due to sharing an extensive degree of overlap with existing measures of personality such that the independent and unique nature of the construct is compromised (Davies, Stankov, & Roberts, 1998).

These models include those that use sets of rating scales similar to those used in personality measures. The two most significant models in this category are Bar-On's (1997) model of emotional and social intelligence and Dulewicz and Higgs' (2003) model of leader emotional intelligence. Bar-On (1997) defines EI as "an array of non-cognitive capabilities, competences, and skills that influence one's ability to succeed in coping with environmental demands and pressures (p.16)." Bar-On's (1997) model includes five components of emotional intelligence, with each dimension labeled as follows: (1) intrapersonal, (2) interpersonal, (3) adaptability, (4) stress management, and (5) general mood. The first area, intrapersonal skills, includes skills of emotional self-awareness, assertiveness, self-regard, self-actualization, and independence. Individuals who possess these skills are able to recognize and understand their own feelings, express their feelings, appraise themselves accurately, realize their potential, and think and act in a self-directed manner without being emotionally dependent on others. The second dimension of interpersonal skills includes skills related to interpersonal relationships, social responsibility, and empathy. Individuals with significant skills are able to establish and maintain mutual and emotionally close relationships and appreciate the feelings of others. The third EI dimension in this model is adaptability and includes skills in problem solving, reality testing, and flexibility. The fourth dimension involves stress management and includes skills related to stress tolerance and impulse control. Finally, the fifth dimension addresses general mood and includes measures of happiness and optimism. Bar-On's instrument to measure EI, Emotional Quotient Inventory (EQ-i) was developed in 1997 (Bar-On, 2004). The EQ-i is designed using a five-point scale ranging from *not true of me* to *true of me* on the scale, which is comprised of 133 items to obtain a total emotional quotient (EQ), based on five main components of Bar-On model: intrapersonal EQ, interpersonal EQ, adaptability EQ, stress management EQ, and general mood EQ.

The second model in this category is the EI model developed by Dulewicz and Higgs (2003). These authors presented a set of 15 competences which they considered to be associated with leadership effectiveness, grouped into three categories: emotional, managerial, and intellectual. Here they identified seven emotional competences comprising emotional intelligence as (1) motivation, (2) conscientiousness, (3) sensitivity, (4) influence, (5) self-awareness, (6) emotional resilience, and (7) intuitiveness. Similar to Bar-On's model previously mentioned, the EI model includes aspects that are similar to existing measures of personality. For example, Bar-On's model includes optimism, while Dulewicz and Higgs' model include conscientiousness. These models therefore integrate both aspects of emotional intelligence that are more similar to a set of character traits or personality dispositions (Petrides & Furnham, 2003) as well as sets of competences or skills that also include noncognitive dimensions, such as stress tolerance (Bar-On, 1997) and motivation (Dulewicz & Higgs, 2003).

2.2.3 Competence Models of Emotional Intelligence

The most widely known competence model of emotional intelligence is that based on Goleman's (1995, 1998) earlier work on emotional intelligence. In this model, EI is defined as "the capacity for recognizing our own feelings and those of others, for motivating ourselves, and for managing emotions effectively in ourselves and others," and emotional competences as "a learned capacity based on EI that contributes to effective performance at work" (Sala, 2006). This formed the basis for the development of the Emotional Competence Inventory (ECI), which proposes that emotional intelligence comprises four competency clusters pertaining to personal and social competence. Goleman's (1998) original theoretical model included five EI constructs: (1) self-awareness, (2) self-regulation, (3) self-motivation, (4) empathy, and (5) social skills. Later, Goleman and colleagues (Goleman, Boyatzis, & McKee, 2002) extended the earlier model and presented a model containing 18 competences, grouping these into four cluster areas: self-awareness, self-management, social awareness, and relationship management. The four competence clusters are defined as follows: (1) *self-awareness* is the ability to read one's emotions and recognize their impact while using gut feelings to guide decisions; (2) *self-management* involves controlling one's emotions and impulses and adapting to changing circumstances; (3) *social awareness* includes the ability to sense, understand, and react to others' emotions while comprehending social networks; and (4) *relationship management* is the ability to inspire, influence, and develop others while managing conflict. Both self- and peer-assessed measures of these competences are obtained with generally a 360-degree assessment being advocated to provide an overall measure of emotional intelligence.

2.2.4 Limitations with Differing Models

These differing models of emotional intelligence that are used in researching emotional intelligence and underpinning developmental interventions, can cause much confusion to those new to the topic. It is important to differentiate between them, however, as the concept of emotional intelligence is perceived rather differently. Although all the models contain a focus on emotional awareness, some of them diverge significantly by also including many other aspects that individuals argue are not technically part of emotional intelligence. For example, aspects of motivation that are contained in the mixed models are thought by many not to be a valid component of emotional intelligence itself, although clearly it may be important in terms of individuals deciding to use their emotional intelligence. For some, the additional components contained in these models invalidate their use. Further, these differing models also reflect more fundamental disagreements among researchers as to whether emotional intelligence is fundamentally similar to an intelligence or to an aspect of personality. The uses of differing models by researchers, therefore, tends to reflect their positions on how they view the nature of emotional intelligence (Bar-On, 1997; Goleman, 1995; Mayer & Salovey, 1997; Schutte et al., 1997; Dulewicz, Higgs, & Slaski, 2003). However, a number of authors have pointed out significant limitations with both competence and mixed model conceptualizations of emotional intelligence.

There are perhaps two major criticisms that are targeted at the use of these models of EI. The first of these concerns is the significant overlap shared with measures based upon these models and existing measures of personality. This means that, although they are useful in directing us to aspects of personality that might be associated with emotional functioning, they may not in themselves represent a *new and independent* construct (Zeidner, Matthews, & Roberts, 2004). For example, a number of studies have shown Bar-On's (1997) EQ-i measure to have strong associations with measures of personality and, in some cases, on all five dimensions (Brackett & Mayer, 2003; Dawda & Hart, 2000; Newsome, Day, & Catano, 2000). This contrasts with findings examining the validity of the MSCEIT, which is the performance-based test designed to measure emotional abilities; in this construct, correlations with personality have been far more moderate (Brackett & Mayer, 2003; O'Connor & Little, 2003).

The second major concern relates to the use of self-report scales to measure EI competences or abilities. These rely upon self endorsements of descriptive statements about individuals, which have been found to have low validity. Self reports of general intelligence compared to actual ability test results have generally been found to weakly correlate ($r = 0.00$ to 0.35) (Paulus, Lysy, & Yik, 1998). Research has also similarly found that self-report EI and actual performance-based measures of EI share little variance ($r = 0.15$ to 0.31) (Mayer, Salovey, & Caruso, 2004), suggesting that these measures tap into separate, independent constructs (Goldenberg, Matheson, & Mantler, 2006). Some concerns remain with the use of performance-based tests for ability conceptualizations of emotional intelligence. For example, whether it actually measures knowledge of appropriate responses rather than one's actual capacity to implement these responses in real life or whether there is indeed a set of correct answers for an emotional intelligence test (Davies, Stankov, & Roberts, 1998; Roberts, Zeidner, & Matthews, 2001). Generally there has been far more widespread support for the validity of the ability model and its corresponding measure of emotional intelligence as opposed to other conceptualizations (Brackett & Mayer, 2003; O'Connor & Little, 2003). Despite limitations with a number of these models, a number of studies have, to date, been conducted which have shown some predictive validity of emotional intelligence with a range of important behaviors suggesting the importance of the concept for projects.

2.3 Emotional Intelligence and Projects: Findings From Relevant Research

2.3.1 Emotional Intelligence in Teams

There has been a significant amount of research over the past decade that has provided significant support for the notion that emotional intelligence may be an important area of individual difference which underpins an individual's capacity to engage in social interactions or an individual's level of social skills (Fox & Spector, 2000; Lopes, Salovey, & Strauss, 2003; Mayer, Roberts, & Barsade, 2008). Indeed a number of studies have demonstrated significant relationships between emotional intelligence and a wide range of social interaction measures (Brackett, Mayer, & Warner, 2004; Lopes et al., 2004). Theoretically such relationships are to be expected based upon a functional perspective of emotions that recognize the important role played in helping us to both communicate our intentions and to understand others' motivations, wants, and desires (Keltner & Haidt, 2001). It is against the background of such developments that a number of writers have considered that emotional intelligence may be particularly advantageous in the context of team working. To date, twelve empirical studies have appeared in the literature that have offered some key insights into the role that emotional intelligence may play in the effectiveness of teams, although the use of differing measures of emotional intelligence in these studies does make direct comparisons between studies difficult. A number of authors have found relationships between emotional intelligence and behaviors or individual dispositions considered important for working in teams and team processes. Rapisarda (2002), in a study of 18 teams of MBA students, found that emotional competences were positively associated with team cohesiveness while Ilarda & Findlay (2006), in a survey of 134 employees, found emotional intelligence was also positively associated with an individual's positive team orientation. Clarke (forthcoming) found that the ability model of emotional intelligence was positively associated with teamwork behaviors important to interpersonal and transition team processes. Emotional intelligence was also found to be associated with leader emergence in a team (Wolff, Pescosolido, & Druskat, 2002).

Other studies have assessed emotional intelligence at the team level, rather than individual level, and also found some very encouraging findings. Feyerherm & Rice (2002), for example, found that a composite measure of emotional intelligence from differing teams was positively associated with managers' ratings of team performance. Similarly three studies by Jordan and his colleagues have found significant positive relationships between team level measures of emotional intelligence and measures of team effectiveness (Jordan, Ashkansay, & Hartel, 2002; Jordan & Troth, 2004; Jordan & Ashkanasy, 2006). Using a similar team-derived measure of EI, Ayoko, Callan, and Hartel (2008), in a study of 122 teams, demonstrated positive relationships between team levels of emotional intelligence and less task and relationship conflict. Clarke (2007a), presenting findings from a qualitative study of student project teams, has also suggested that team members' emotional intelligence may play an important role in facilitating critical reflection and team learning, which corresponds with more recent research suggesting emotional intelligence may play a role in underpinning knowledge transfer mechanisms within projects (Decker, Landceta, & Kotnour 2009). Additional studies have also found positive relationships with both team level measures of emotional intelligence and team performance indices (Koman & Wolff, 2008; Offerman et al., 2004).

2.3.2 Emotional Intelligence and Leadership

Given the increasing prominence of the "soft" or human side of project management, it is not surprising that there has emerged a significant focus on project leadership as a key area of activity through which project managers engage in and achieve their goals in relationship management (Norrie & Walker, 2004; Pinto et al., 1998; Thambain, 2004). Key aspects of the work in this area, to date, have been attempts to identify how project leadership behaviors differ from other aspects of the project manager's role (Norrie & Walker, 2004; Turner, 1999; Verma 1996), and to show how different leadership styles may be appropriate for either differing types (Crawford, Hobbs, & Turner, 2005; Turner & Muller, 2005 Prabhakar, 2006) or life cycle stages in a project (Lee Kelley, Leong, & Loong, 2003; Muller & Turner, 2007). Key findings from some of this research has been a recognition of both considerate leadership behaviors (Stogdill, 1974) and transformational leadership (Bass & Avolio, 1994; Bass, 1998) as important leadership styles that project managers need as part of their skill set, given the significant role they play in motivating and inspiring project team members.

Importantly, a number of authors have argued that emotional intelligence is likely to underpin such leadership qualities (Carmeli, 2003; Daus & Ashkanasy, 2005; George, 2000; Prati et al., 2003). Many of the arguments are based on an increasing recognition that leadership is intrinsically an emotional process (Megerian & Sosik, 1996). Previous perspectives on leadership tended to focus purely on the cognitive and behavioral dimensions of leadership, and generally ignored this important aspect of the leadership relationship (George, 2000). A growing body of research however has been building, which shows that leaders, who are better able to recognize the emotional states of their followers and promote more positive emotional states in the teams they lead, are often effective within contemporary organizational settings (Humphrey 2002).

Importantly leadership practices that foster positive affectivity have been found to be associated with important job and work-related outcomes. Both Pirola-Merlo, Hartel, Mann, and Hirst (2002) and Sy, Cote, and Saavedra (2005), for example, have found that increased team performance was associated with team leaders fostering positive team climates. McColl-Kennedy and Anderson (2002) showed that transformational leadership behaviors helped employees to feel more optimistic and deal more effectively with frustrating events at work. More recently, Ozcelik, Langton, and Aldrich (2008) found that leadership practices which were linked to creating a positive emotional climate were associated with organizational performance. George (2000) described in detail how emotional intelligence might be expected to be associated with these leadership processes. She suggests, for example, that leaders who are able to effectively appraise and manage emotions, are able to generate far more compelling visions for their followers, resulting in higher levels of motivation. Connecting on an emotional level with followers is also thought central to developing higher levels of trust and commitment (Jones & George, 1998; Sosik & Megerian, 1999). Leban and Zulauf (2004) suggest that project managers who understand the moods and emotions of stakeholders can help them to make better decisions about how strategies should be presented and therefore are able to gain greater goal acceptance from followers.

Empirical findings are also supporting a relationship between emotional intelligence and leadership. Barling, Slater, and Kelloway (2000) found EI to be associated with three characteristics of transformational leadership—namely, idealized influence, individualized consideration and inspirational motivation. Palmer, Walls, Burgess, and Stough (2001), who used the modified Trait Meta Mood Scale (TMMS), a self-report measure of emotional intelligence that captures an individual's ability to monitor and manage their emotions, also found a relationship with the idealized influence and individualized consideration dimensions of transformational leadership. Similarly, Gardner and Stough (2002) found that the ability to perceive and understand emotion in others, in particular, was significantly associated with individualized consideration, in addition to a significant relationship between transformational leadership and overall emotional intelligence scores. More recently, Rosete and Ciarrochi (2005) also found positive findings when they examined the relationship between emotional intelligence and indices of leadership performance in an Australian public service organization using ability measures of emotional intelligence. Following on from this research, the potential significance of emotional intelligence for effectively leading projects becomes apparent. However it has been suggested that there are additional factors associated with projects specifically that place further emphasis on a particular role for emotional intelligence.

2.3.3 Emotional Intelligence and Projects

Over recent years there has become a "projectification" of work practices, referring to the extent to which project management as a form of work organization has been adopted in areas far beyond the traditional areas of construction, engineering, and information systems. More contemporary writings now recognize the spread of project management throughout a myriad of industries and sectors, including the creative industries, health care, and professional services, to name but a few (Turner & Keegan, 1999). With increasing applications being found for project management, combined with the need for project management to respond to changing business environments, the knowledge and skill base that underpins project management has continued to evolve. This has pushed the boundaries of knowledge and skills required beyond what has often been the more traditional focus on technical and administrative procedures and systems that are associated with project management. Such changes, however, have posed their own challenges, not least in the attempts to identify the appropriate competences to now underpin project management practice (Crawford, Morris, Thomas, & Winter, 2006; Thirty, 2004; Winter & Thomas, 2004).

Hodgson and Cicmil (2006), in identifying the limitations with the traditional knowledge base that has underpinned project management, point to its beginning to evolve in order to better understand the "actuality" of projects. The authors use this term to convey the extent to which the traditional concerns of both research and training in project management may be becoming increasingly detached from the lived experience and challenges arising from working in contemporary projects. In particular, they draw attention to the increasing importance of skill sets for project management that need to accommodate a far greater focus on the following:

(1) Controlling the performance of projects—that is, enforcing the particular set of actions project actors are required to undertake in order to produce the desired outcome by managing the motivations and actions of people.
(2) Managing relationships among people—that is, managing the whole "system" of interrelated roles and tasks and their interconnectedness.
(3) Managing the project team culture through project leadership—that is, designing and controlling the system of values and beliefs in order to motivate people to subscribe to identified goals.
(4) Designing and managing the learning process of project members.
(5) Capturing, managing, and transferring knowledge in project environments.

To some extent, this is in response to an increasing recognition that difficulties, and in some instances, failures that are frequently encountered in projects, are located in many of the key areas identified previously. Given the shift in emphasis to the relational management aspects of working in projects, together with recent research showing relationships between emotional intelligence in related areas, it is perhaps not surprising that some attention has now been directed to question as to the role that emotional intelligence may play in assisting project managers to work more effectively in these changing project environments. Druskat and Druskat (2006) for example, have suggested that the particular nature and characteristics of projects may well mean that emotional intelligence is of even more importance within this specific work arena than within more traditional forms of the work organization. Specifically, they highlight how the nature of effective project working places emphasize particular attributes of project workers that are highly likely to be underpinned by emotional intelligence. They draw attention to four key aspects in particular:

1) The temporary nature of projects. Given that projects are mostly formed around finite time spans, this requires project workers to be able to quickly form and facilitate good interpersonal relationships at the outset of each new project. Time pressures mean that the pattern of relationship building does not mirror other types of teams. For project managers, it means that aspects of projects found to be associated with successful working, such as trust and commitment which arise through interpersonal interaction, also need to be quickly established (Kloppenborg & Petrick 1999; Sweeney & Lee, 1999). Further, the nature of the project team does not mirror traditional teams but is characterized as more typically organic or "loose" subject to rapidly changing membership as expertise enters and leaves the project as required

(Briner, Geddes, & Hastings, 1990). Emotional competences that underpin effective communication and social skills are therefore likely to be of major significance.

2) Projects are Unique. Each fresh, new project will involve new challenges that require to be addressed quickly without the benefit of learning from established or repetitive routines. Failure to identify and address these challenges in time may seriously jeopardize the success of the project. Similarly there is now far greater acknowledgement of the complexity associated with managing projects arising from their temporary and unique goal oriented characteristics (Frame, 1995). Again, emotional competences that underpin the building and consolidation of interpersonal relationships between project members as well as stakeholders should facilitate greater knowledge exchange between members and therefore increased likelihood of learning required to deal with uncertainty.

3) Projects involve Change. Both the increasing complexity associated with projects and the uncertainty it generates inevitably means that effectively managing change is critical to project work (Briner, Geddes, & Hasting, 1990; Slevin & Pinto, 1991). Change evokes significant emotions ranging from excitement to anxiety, frustration, and even anger. Effectively managing these emotions plays a significant role in determining whether positive emotions are channelled into productive behaviors, or whether negative emotions stifle effective teamworking, leave individuals impotent, or, worse still, degenerate into increasing self-serving sets of behaviors that may pose a risk to project success. Makilouko (2004), for example, argued that project managers needed emotional capacity in order to channel the stress caused in dealing with the ambiguity of multicultural situations. Effective leadership during change is paramount where emotional competences, which enable a project manager to inspire fellow project workers and motivate them towards change, play a significant role.

4) Increased Cross-Cultural Project Work. The very fact that projects nearly always involve a coalition of different organizations sometimes from different countries but nearly always involving parties from a wide range of differing professional backgrounds, brings unique challenges for working in projects. Inevitably there is considerable scope for misunderstanding and miscommunication arising from cultural differences, which can cause serious problems if not managed effectively. Emotional competences such as empathy and those associated with self-awareness, are seen as key strengths when working in projects that underpin attentive behavior and interpersonal understanding, which can play a role in minimizing such misunderstandings or enabling difficulties to be resolved should they arise.

Each of these aforementioned factors present compelling arguments for why emotional intelligence may be of particular relevance for project teams not just because they are teams, but, more significantly, because they are projects. To date, however, few studies have appeared in the literature that have specifically examined the role of emotional intelligence within project contexts. In particular, no studies have examined relationships between emotional intelligence and those specific project management competences posited to be important in those areas suggested by Druskat and Druskat (2006) for successful project outcomes. Furthermore, few studies have appeared in the literature that have specifically used ability-based measures of emotional intelligence as opposed to mixed-model or competence measures of EI which have often been criticized as having less validity. Given suggestions that emotional intelligence is associated with project management effectiveness, it follows that there is also a need to determine whether emotional intelligence, perceived as a set of emotional abilities, is amenable to development. This being the case, a pilot research project comprising two separate studies was undertaken in order to further our understanding of the role that emotional intelligence may play in projects. The research project was undertaken with project managers in the UK and sought to address the following objectives:

(1) Identify the relationships between emotional intelligence abilities and specific project management competences associated with effective project management.
(2) Identify relationships between emotional intelligence abilities and transformational leadership behaviors.
(3) Identify whether training can result in improvements in project managers' emotional intelligence abilities and relevant project manager competences.
(4) Identify factors that may be associated with the effectiveness of emotional intelligence training.
(5) Develop a range of training materials that might be used in future training programs targeting project managers' emotional intelligence.

The following two sections detail findings from two studies that were conducted to address the first two objectives and then the following two objectives respectively. Section five discusses the implications of the findings from both of these studies and considers areas for future research. Section six details the theoretical underpinnings of the training intervention that was undertaken. Finally, section seven contains the training materials that were specifically developed for use on the training program.

SECTION 3.0

Study One: The Relationship Between Emotional Intelligence Abilities, Project Management Competences, and Transformational Leadership Behaviors

3.1   Introduction

Given that the interest in the concept of emotional intelligence is rather a recent phenomenon, it is surprising that the importance of emotionally associated abilities or skills in project management was recognized over three decades ago. Hill (1977) identified how high-performing project managers were more likely to adopt greater listening and coaching behaviors, as well as facilitate openness and emotional expression. More recently, these skills or abilities have again been the focus of attention within project management, driven by the wider research in emotional intelligence and the increasing literature voicing concerns over the appropriate knowledge and skill base required for effective project management (Crawford, Morris, Thomas & Winter, 2006; El-Sabaa, 2001; Sizemore, 1988; Zimmerer & Yasin, 1998). Writers such as Winter et al. (2006), for example, have suggested that emotional competences are associated with the intuition and skills necessary for project managers to become reflective practitioners. As a result, project managers with high emotional intelligence should be better equipped to solve new challenges and problems that each new project brings. There have also been concerns that the training offered to project managers remains heavily weighted towards the hard, technical skills of the role, while the human skills have received far less attention (Pant & Baroudi, 2008). Although there is a growing body of research into the role that emotional intelligence plays in teams and in underpinning effective leadership, both of which are highly relevant for project working, the literature specifically examining emotional intelligence in projects is only just emerging.

In terms of empirical work investigating the role of emotional intelligence specifically in projects, our knowledge in this area remains fairly limited. Findings from recent studies examining emotional intelligence within a project management context would appear to confirm findings from studies more widely in the leadership literature that have found emotional intelligence to be a significant area of individual difference associated with effective leadership and, more specifically, transformational leadership (Butler & Chinowsky, 2006; Leban & Zulauf, 2004; Muller & Turner, 2007; Sunindijo, Hadikusumo, & Ogunlansa, 2007). However, a significant limitation of these studies is that, in either instance, there was no attempt to control for personality effects. Given that the measures of emotional intelligence used in almost every case (c.f. Leban & Zulauf, 2004) have received criticism for sharing some overlap with existing measures of personality, it becomes difficult to isolate the actual contribution that emotional intelligence may be making in relation to its underpinning particular behaviors or competences considered important for working in projects.

Given these limitations, this study aims to make a contribution to our understanding of the role emotional intelligence may play in projects by presenting findings from a pilot study that examined relationships between emotional intelligence, project management competences, and transformational leadership. Importantly, this study is an advance on previous research in this area by specifically controlling for both cognitive ability and personality. In so doing, the actual contribution of emotional intelligence in explaining variation in particular project management behaviors can be more clearly determined. The study is also the first to specifically identify which areas of project management practice, as outlined by current perspectives on project manager competences, are likely to be influenced by emotional intelligence using an ability measure of the construct. Given criticisms of other EI models that have been used in research to date within the project management field, this again offers a more targeted focus for identifying the specific contribution emotional intelligence may make within a project management context. Based on a sample of project managers in the UK, the findings suggest that emotional intelligence abilities and empathy may be a significant aspect of individual difference that contributes to behaviors associated with competences in the areas of teamwork, attentiveness, and managing conflict in projects.

3.2 Findings From Previous Studies Examining Emotional Intelligence in Projects

To date, only five studies have appeared in the literature specifically investigating emotional intelligence in project contexts, all of which have examined relationships

Table 1. Summary of Published Studies Examining Emotional Intelligence and Projects

Authors	Study	EI Measure	Dependent Measures	Results
Leban & Zulauf (2004)	24 project managers drawn from different industries	MSCEIT (ability)	Transformational leadership (MLQ)	Total emotional intelligence scores were associated with inspirational motivation
Mount (2005)	74 asset construction project managers	ECI (peer)	Project management skills	Positive relationship between ECI and project manager skills for successful projects
Butler & Chinowsky (2006)	130 engineering executives	EQ-i (self report)	Transformational leadership (MLQ-5)	Positive relationship between total EQ and transformational leadership
Sunindijo et al. (2007)	34 project manager and project engineers (PMEs)	ECI-based measure	Leadership behaviors identified from literature	PMEs with high EI scores used more leadership behaviors—e.g., stimulating, rewarding, delegating, open communication, listening, participating
Muller & Turner (2007)	400 project management professionals	EIQ (self report)	Project type/ Project complexity	Positive relationships found between a number of emotional competences and project characteristics

between emotional intelligence and either leadership or project management competences Table 1). Four of these studies examined leadership in projects. Leban and Zulauf (2004) conducted a study of 24 project managers from six different organizations drawn from a wide range of industries. Data on the project manager's leadership style was obtained from team members and stakeholders, while the Mayer-Salovey-Caruso-Emotional Intelligence Ability Test (MSCEIT; Mayer & Salovey 1997) was used to assess the emotional intelligence of project managers. Overall emotional intelligence scores and the ability to understand emotions were found to be significantly related with the inspirational motivation dimension of transformational leadership.

Butler and Chinowsky (2006) investigated the relationship between emotional intelligence and leadership among senior level (vice-president or above) construction executives; however, this study used Bar-On's (1997) model of emotional intelligence, the EQ-i. This is a multifactorial model of emotional, personal, and social abilities that include the five EI domains of interpersonal skills, intrapersonal skills, adaptability, stress management, and general mood. Collecting data from 130 executives, they found a significant relationship between the total EQ-I score and transformational leadership. Of significance, this accounted for 34% of the variance of transformational leadership behavior. Of all the emotional intelligence dimensions they examined, interpersonal skills were found to be the most significant.

Muller & Turner (2007) sought to determine whether different types of leadership were more important depending upon the type of project. In a survey of 400 project management professionals, they identified which sorts of leadership competences were associated with success in different project types. Their overall results point to the variegated nature of leadership and how different sets of competences are appropriate for leadership in projects depending upon its degree of complexity (high, medium, or low), and the application area (e.g., engineering and construction, information systems, business). However, they used an additional model of emotional intelligence to underpin their study, drawing upon Dulewicz and Higgs' (2003) 15 leadership competences. Within this EI model, 15 leadership competences are identified. Seven of these competences are categorized as emotional leadership competences which encompass (1) motivation, (2) conscientiousness, (3) sensitivity, (4) influence, (5) self-awareness, (6) emotional resilience, and (7) intuitiveness. Among their results, they found that the leadership competences of emotional resilience and communication accounted for most success in projects of medium complexity, while the emotional competency of sensitivity was found to be most important for high complexity projects. They also found that the emotional competency of conscientiousness was associated with success throughout all stages of the life cycle of projects. Different competences were also found to be associated with greater success, dependent upon the application area in which the project was based. For example, the emotional competences of conscientiousness and motivation were found to be most important for engineering projects, while self-awareness alongside communication was most important in information systems projects. Together the findings are significant in that they suggest differing leadership styles may be associated with varying project contexts. Further, also that differing emotional competences drawn from the EI model they used, are associated with each of the differing leadership styles. They concluded that project managers who possess a wider set of these emotional intelligence competences are more likely to be able to adopt their styles and behaviors to differing project conditions.

Finally, Sunindijo, Hadikusumo, and Ogunlansa (2007) investigated the relationship between emotional intelligence competences and leadership styles in 54 projects based in Bangkok. They identified 13 leadership behaviors from the literature and collected usable data on four dimensions of emotional intelligence from 30 project managers and engineers (PMEs). They also collected data on their leadership behaviors from their supervisors. This time, they used a fourth differing model of emotional intelligence to underpin their study, an instrument they obtained commercially which they suggest was based upon Goleman's (1995) EI competency model. Their results showed that those PMEs with higher EI mean scores demonstrated a greater frequency in the use of key leadership behaviors compared to PMEs with low EI scores. This included behaviors such as stimulating, rewarding, delegating, leading by example, open communication, listening, participating, and proactive behavior. However, it is important to note that statistically significant differences were only found for the leadership behavior of open communication and proactive behavior, and these were both at the 10% level of significance.

The final study, located in the literature in this area, focused instead on examining relationships between emotional intelligence and project management competences. Mount (2006) presented results from a study that was designed to identify the job competences that were associated with superior performance in a major international petroleum corporation. Using a range of data collection techniques including focus groups, interviews, surveys, as well as data from critical incidents, data were collected on job roles performed among other staff groups on74 asset construction project managers. The roles these project managers occupied was under transition, moving from a traditional engineering role to one that was more strategically aligned to individual business units. Using Goleman's (1995) set of emotional competences, they found that seven emotional competences (influence, self-confidence, teamwork, organizational awareness, adaptability, empathy, and achievement motivation), accounted for 69% of the skill set these project managers considered to be the most significant for their success on projects.

Together these studies suggest a significant role for emotional intelligence in terms of underpinning both leadership and important behaviors that have been suggested as associated with successful outcomes in projects. Supporting findings obtained from the wider literature, emotional intelligence in these studies was found to be significantly associated with dimensions of transformational leadership. Previously, transformational leadership had been found to be associated with significant performance in organizations (Lowe, Kroeck, & Sivasubramiam 1996; Yammarino, Spangler, & Bass 1993), and had also been suggested as the most appropriate leadership style for project management given its close association with leading successful change (Herold, Fedor, Caldwell, & Liu, 2008; Leban & Zulauf, 2004). However these EI and project studies do suffer a number of major limitations. The first of these relates to criticisms associated with the validity of the particular EI measures used. Both Goleman's and Bar-On's measures of emotional intelligence used in two of the EI project studies discussed earlier contain a number of dimensions (such as achievement, motivation, and organizational awareness in relation to the former; and assertiveness, stress management, and general mood in relation to the latter), which have been argued as technically not falling within the EI domain. The use of such measures to capture emotional intelligence have led a number of authors to raise serious doubts as to whether these conceptualizations and measures of EI are able to offer anything new over other existing measures already well known in the literature (Conte, 2005; Locke, 2005). Instead, the ability model of emotional intelligence and its associated measure have received far greater support as offering a more valid and conceptually distinct approach to considering the EI construct (Brackett & Mayer, 2003; O'Connor & Little, 2003). Studies using this measure of EI within the project management field may therefore be able to more clearly delineate the specific contribution of emotional intelligence.

A further significant limitation of these studies is that there was no attempt to control for either general ability or personality. In terms of individual differences, cognitive ability is widely recognized as perhaps the most important predictor of performance across a wide range of job contexts (Schmidt & Hunter 1998). In terms of leadership too, cognitive abilities have been found to be significant predictors of leadership performance (Antonakis, 2003; Judge, Bono, Ilies, & Gerhardt, 2002). Leadership, like project management, involves many behaviors that are likely associated with its effectiveness. However emotional intelligence is likely to be more relevant depending upon how far the particular behaviors associated with leadership and competences in project management involve getting things done through people relationships (Jordan & Troth, 2004; Offerman, Bailey, Vasilopoulos, Seal, & Sass, 2004). A number of writers have argued that the significance of emotional intelligence, particularly in leadership, is dependent upon leadership that is seen fundamentally as a relational activity (Prati, Douglas, Ferrus, Ammeter, & Buckley, 2003; Zhou & George, 2003). It is therefore important that studies control for both cognitive ability and personality, if the additional contribution EI makes is to be determined. For example, the emotional competence of conscientiousness found to be significant for leadership in differing project types and complexity by Muller and Turner (2007) may well be tapping into the similarly named personality factor found in the Big 5 (McCrae & Costa, 1987).

We are also still some way from gathering findings from research specifically within the project management field, that may lend support for key arguments outlined earlier by Druskat and Druskat (2006) suggesting why EI may be particularly important within project contexts. Despite the limitations from the use of the particular EI measure used, Mount's (2006) study, which examines the relationship between emotional intelligence and the skills for successful project management, does offer some preliminary signs that emotional intelligence may be important for a wide range of behaviors considered necessary for working in project management contexts. However, to date, no studies have yet to appear in the literature that have examined relationships between emotional intelligence and those specific behaviors suggested as significant by Druskat and Druskat (2006) as key to working in projects.

3.3 Focus of the Current Study

Given the limitations with some of the previous studies examining emotional intelligence in projects, this study seeks to build on the current literature in two major ways: (a) through investigating whether emotional intelligence is associated with a number of behaviors posited as key for successfully working in project contexts; and (b) by using an ability-based model of emotional intelligence and controlling for both cognitive ability and personality.

Regarding the investigation of whether emotional intelligence is associated with a number of behaviors as key for successfully working in project contexts, Druskat and

Druskat (2006) suggested that the specific characteristics of projects are unique from other forms of work organization that place an additional premium on the importance of emotional intelligence. They identified four specific characteristics alongside specific project manager behaviors that are necessary for successful project management. Firstly, the temporary nature of projects places considerable emphasis on communication skills. Secondly, the uniqueness of every project requires well-developed teamwork skills. Thirdly, the complexity of projects requires highly developed skills to involve other project members and respond to their concerns. Finally, the requirements for inter-organizational and international collaboration associated with many projects requires skills in cross-cultural management, particularly those relating to conflict management. However much of this has yet to receive any empirical support based upon research in projects.

This first component of the pilot study therefore sought to address the following two objectives:

(1) To identify the relationships between emotional intelligence abilities and specific project manager competences identified as critical within project contexts.
(2) To identify relationships between emotional intelligence and transformational leadership behaviors.

Five specific hypotheses were tested in the study to address these two objectives. Each of these and their rationales are included herein. Teamwork skills have been identified in a number of studies as among the "critical success factors" of projects (Rudolph, Wagner, & Fawcett, 2008; Tisher, Dvir, Shenhar, & Lipovetsky, 1996). Many authors have suggested that emotional intelligence is either responsible for, or underpins an individual's ability to engage in social interactions (Caruso & Wolfe, 2001; Lopes, Salovey, & Strauss, 2003) such that it may well be an underlying construct of social skills (Fox & Spector, 2000). This is based on the premise that emotions are key components of both how we communicate and can facilitate socialization within groups (Keltner & Haidt, 2001; Lopes et al., 2004). Supporting this proposition have been a number of studies which have demonstrated significant relationships between EI measures and a range of social interaction indices, including more positive social interactions with peers and friends (Brackett, Mayer & Warner, 2004). Individuals scoring higher on the emotional ability to manage emotions, for example, have reported more satisfying interpersonal relationships (Lopes et al., 2003). Elsewhere, research examining emotional intelligence within a team context has found positive relationships between EI and propensity for teamwork (Ilarda & Findlay, 2006) and EI and interpersonal team processes (Clarke, in press). This, therefore, leads to the first hypothesis:

Hypothesis 1: Emotional intelligence abilities and empathy will be positively associated with the project management competence of teamwork.

Differences in individuals' emotional skills have long been suggested as accounting for variations in the extent to which they are able to decode nonverbal and emotional communication (Friedman & Riggio, 1981; Hall & Bernieri, 2001; Riggio, 1986; Rosenthal, 1979). Both emotional intelligence abilities and empathy have been identified as underpinning more effective communication (Ickes, 1997; Riggio, Riggio, Salinas, & Cole, 2003). Project manager communication skills and the quality of communication in projects have been found to contribute to project outcomes (Drouin, Bourgault, & Bartholomew-Saunders, 2008) Previously, Sunindijo, Hadikusumo, and Ogunlana (2007) found a positive relationship between emotional intelligence competences and project manager competences that included communication. This gives rise to the second hypothesis:

Hypothesis 2: Emotional intelligence abilities and empathy will be positively associated with the project management competence of communication.

Addressing the individual needs and concerns of team members and involving them in decisions have long been recognized as key aspects associated with team effectiveness (Dyer, 1995) and important behaviors associated with effective leadership of teams (Adair, 1979; Fleishman, 1974). These attentiveness behaviors have been identified as important for relationship building, social integration, enhancing group identification, and developing commitment and trust, all seen as key elements associated with the effectiveness of teams (Bishop & Scott, 2000; Cohen & Bailey, 1997). More recently these behavioral dimensions of project managers have also been suggested as important to success in projects (Drouin et al., 2008; Dvir, Ben-David, Sadeh, & Shenhar, 2006; Lester, 1998; Randolph & Posner, 1988; Strohmeier, 1992; Taborda, 2000). These attentiveness behaviors are likely to assist project managers to build high-quality inter-personal relationships within short periods of time, which is important given the unique and temporary nature of projects (Druskat & Druskat, 2006). Emotional sensitivity and emotional expression are key aspects associated with emotional intelligence and empathy that have been suggested as associated with performing attentiveness behaviors (Feyerherm & Rice, 2002; Rapisarda, 2002; Riggio & Reichard, 2008). Previous research has also found a positive relationship between the two emotional abilities, using emotions to facilitate thinking and managing emotions and attentiveness behaviors associated with interpersonal team processes (Clarke, forthcoming). This give rise to the third hypothesis:

Hypothesis 3: Emotional intelligence abilities and empathy will be positively associated with the project management competence of attentiveness.

Conflict between partners and members has often been cited as a major factor undermining effectiveness or contributing to failure in projects (Nordin, 2006; Sommerville & Langford, 1994; Terje & Hakansson, 2003) and is widely recognized as a consistent feature associated with working in projects (Lazlo & Goldberg,

2008; Terje, 2004). Previous research has found relationships between emotional intelligence and better conflict management strategies in team settings (Ayoko, Callan & Hartel, 2008; Jordan & Troth, 2004); however, these studies used team level measures. Rahim and Psenicka (2002) reported findings which examine emotional intelligence and conflict management strategies at the individual level using Goleman's model (1998) of EI. They found that self-awareness was associated with self-regulation and empathy. Empathy was associated with Goleman's motivation measure, which in turn was positively associated with more effective approaches to conflict management. A positive relationship between self-regulation and the use of positive approaches to managing conflict have also been found using a trait measure of EI (Kausahal & Kwanters, 2006). Although no studies to date have investigated relationships between emotional intelligence and conflict management using the ability model of emotional intelligence at the individual level, a number of authors have suggested that emotional abilities should assist individuals to better regulate their emotional responses in conflict situations, which would prevent them from spiraling out of control. Similarly, individuals with a better understanding of how circumstances and situations cause both positive and negative emotional responses should be better at recognizing potential conflict flashpoints and successfully dealing with conflict at earlier stages so it might be used more creatively rather than become destructive (Zhou & George 2004). This gives rise to the fourth hypothesis:

> *Hypothesis 4: Emotional intelligence abilities and empathy will be positively associated with the project management competence of conflict management.*

Transformational leadership (Bass & Alvolio, 1994) comprises the four key dimensions of (1) idealized influence, (2) inspirational motivation, (3) intellectual stimulation, and (4) individualized consideration. This type of leadership is associated with higher levels of motivation in the followers through activating their higher-level needs and generating a closer identification between leaders and followers. A number of authors have suggested that underpinning transformational leadership is the enhanced emotional attachment to the leader (Ashkanasy & Tse, 2000; Dulewicz & Higgs, 2003) that arises as a result of leaders using emotional intelligence. By accurately identifying emotions in followers, leaders are able to respond more effectively to their needs. Through expressing emotions effectively, leaders can generate compelling visions for followers and gain greater goal acceptance (George, 2000; Sosik & Megerian, 1999). The use of positive affect can also influence followers' mood states which then impact on different outcomes (Sy, Cote, & Saavedra, 2005). A number of studies previously have found significant relationships between emotional intelligence and transformational leadership (Barling, Slater, & Kelloway, 2000; Downey, Papageorgiou, & Stough, 2005; Mandell and Pherwani, 2003) as well as a number of studies specifically within project contexts (Butler & Chinowsky, 2006; Leban & Zulauf, 2004). This gives rise to the fifth hypothesis:

Hypothesis 5: Emotional intelligence abilities will be positively associated with project management transformational leadership.

3.4 The Study and Methods

Sixty-seven project managers were recruited from two organizations based in the UK and from the UK chapter of the Project Management Institute to take part in the study. Both organizations were actively engaged in projects as their major form of work process. The first was a national arts organization involved in commissioning and developing projects within the cultural sector. The second was a national organization comprising a number of divisions ranging from construction, research and development, and professional services, working across a range of differing business sectors. The average age of participants was 39.6 years (SD 7.9), and ages ranged from 23 to 58 years old. Eighteen of these participants (27%) were qualified in project management. Participants identified their core job function as follows: general management 20 (30%), marketing/sales 2 (3%), HRM/training 3 (4.5%), finance 2 (3%), R&D 2 (3%), technical 6 (9%) and other 32 (47.5%). The relatively large number of participants identified in the other category can be explained by the significant number of participants working in specialist fields in either education or the arts. Table 2 illustrates the nature of project management experience possessed by those taking part in the study. Here we can see that more than half of the participants taking part in the study had experience working in projects associated with organizational change followed by information technology. When asked to describe the degree of complexity associated with these projects, they were usually involved; just over 75% rated these as either medium or high complexity.

3.4.1 Procedure

All participants were asked to complete on-line instruments to assess emotional intelligence, empathy, cognitive ability, personality, transformational leadership, and project management competences within a 2-week period in 2008.

Table 2. Study One—Participants' Experience in Projects

Project Type	Yes	No	Uncertain
Engineering	18 (27%)	48 (72%)	1 (1.5%)
Information Technology	21 (31%)	45 (67%)	1 (1.5%)
Community Development	9 (13%)	52 (78%)	7 (10%)
Organizational Change	38 (57%)	22 (33%)	6 (9%)
Complexity			
High	19 (28%)		
Medium	33 (49%)		
Low	13 (19%)		
Uncertain	2 (4%)		

3.4.2 Measures

3.4.2.1 *Independent Measures:*

(1) Emotional Intelligence. Emotional intelligence was measured using the MSCEIT V2.0 available from MHS Assessments. The MSCEIT V2.0 consists of 141 items divided into eight sections or tasks that correspond with the four branches or abilities of Mayer and Salovey's (1997) ability model of emotional intelligence: (a) perceiving emotions (B1), (b) using emotions to facilitate thinking (B2), (c) understanding Emotions (B3), and (d) managing emotions in oneself and others (B4).

Participants completed the assessment online, and scores for each of the branches were computed by the test administrators (MHS Assessments). Scores were standardized in relation to a normative sample of over 5,000 individuals with a mean of 100 and standard deviation of 15. Reliabilities for the scales were previously reported as 0.90, 0.76, 0.77, 0.81, and 0.91 for each of the four branch scales and the full scale, respectively (Mayer et al., 2002). Reliabilities obtained here for each of the four branches were 0.88, 0.69, 0.90, and 0.55 respectively, and 0.92 for the full scale (total EI).

(2) Empathy. Mehrabian and Epstein's (1972) 33 items of emotional empathy were used to assess empathetic tendency. Responses to each item were scored on a scale ranging from +4 (very strong agreement) to −4 (very strong disagreement). Scores on 17 items were negatively scored in that the signs of a participant's response on negative items were changed. A total empathy score was then obtained by adding all 33 items. Sample items include (1) (+) "It makes me sad to see a lonely stranger in a group," and (24) (−) "I am able to make decisions without being influenced by people's feelings." The scale authors previously reported on the split-half reliability for the measure was 0.84. Here the Spearman-Brown split-half coefficient was found to be 0.82, suggesting good reliability.

3.4.2.2 *Dependent Measures*

(1) Project Manager Competences. An instrument for measuring four project management competences posited to be associated with emotional intelligence was constructed. Each project management competence contained three or more behaviors within an overall scale. Participants were asked to rate how well they performed each behavior in the last project they were involved in. Each item was assessed using a seven-point Likert scale ranging from "1= not at all well" to "7= very well." Scores for each competence were then obtained by adding all relevant behavioral items and then obtaining the mean score for each scale. Details of scale validation are provided below. Sample items for each of the four scales and reliability coefficients obtained are as follows:

A. *Communication* (alpha 0.70). Sample items included (1) understood the communication from others involved in the project; and (2) maintained informal communication channels.

B. *Teamwork* (alpha 0.78). Sample items included (1) helped to build a positive attitude and optimism for success on the project; and (2) helped others to see different points of view or perspectives.

C. *Attentiveness* (alpha 0.68). Sample items included (1) responded to and acted upon expectations, concerns, and issues raised by others in the project; and (2) actively listened to other project team members or stakeholders involved in the project.

D. *Managing Conflict* (alpha 0.86). Sample items included (1) helped to solve relationship issues and problems that emerged on the project; and (2) managed ambiguous situations satisfactorily while supporting the project's goals. All scales were found to have good reliabilities (Nunally & Bernstein, 1993).

(2) Project Managers' Transformational Leadership. The Multifactor Leadership Questionnaire Form 5X (Bass & Avolio, 1997) was used to measure transformational leadership behaviors. All of the MLQ-5X responses are made on a five-point scale ranging from "0 = Not at all" to "4 = Frequently, if not always." Transformational leadership is measured by four subscales: idealized influence, inspirational motivation, intellectual stimulation, and individualized consideration. Items from these subscales were added and then the mean was used to provide a total score for each scale. Previous research has shown good reliability and validity for the total scales and subscales ranging from 0.74 to 0.94 (Bass & Avolio, 2000). Reliabilities for each of the subscales obtained here were 0.68, 0.52, 0.85, and 0.55 for idealized influence, inspirational motivation, intellectual stimulation, and individualized consideration, respectively. Reliability for the overall scale was 0.84.

(3) Control Variables. Control variables were as follows:

A. *Personality.* Personality was assessed using the Individual Perceptions Inventory (IPI; Goldberg, et al., 2006). This is based upon McCrae and Costa's Big 5 personality characteristics and consists of a 50-item questionnaire designed to capture the personality dimensions of extraversion, agreeableness, conscientiousness, emotional stability, and openness. Previous studies have shown the IPI to have strong convergent validity with other personality measures such as the 16PF and the NEO-PI (Goldberg, 1999). Scale reliabilities were found here to be extraversion (0.89), agreeableness (0.83), conscientiousness (0.78), emotional stability (0.84), and openness (0.81).

B. *General Mental Ability.* General Mental Ability (GMA) was measured using the 50-item Wonderlic Personnel Test (WPT; Wonderlic & Associates, 1983). Participants completed the timed test online and a single score was provided, indicative of an individual's overall level of GMA. Reported reliabilities for the Wonderlic test ranged from 0.78 to 0.95 and have been shown to have good convergent validity with other measures of intelligence such as the Wechsler Adult Intelligence Scale (WAIS, Wonderlic & Associates, 1983).

C. *Project Management Qualification.* Previous certification in project management is likely to have familiarized participants with those competences that were being self-assessed in the study and might therefore influence more positive responses. In order to control for the effects of familiarity with project management competences, certification in project management was entered as a further control variable. This was similarly entered as a simple dichotomous coding with "1 = certified in project management" and "0 = not certified."

3.4.3 Procedure for Validation of Project Manager Competence Scales

Clarke (in press) previously suggested that studies should theoretically justify which aspects of behaviors, associated with working in projects or teams, one would expect emotional intelligence to be associated with prior to examining relationships. Druskat and Druskat (2006) put forward arguments suggesting that the characteristics of projects placed particular emphasis on project manager behaviors associated with communication, teamwork, building interpersonal relationships (attentiveness), and managing conflict. Based on the rationales outlined above, significant relationships should be expected between emotional intelligence and these project manager competences. In order to ground behavioral items associated with these competences within project management, items were initially selected from the *Project Manager Competency Development Framework* (PMI, 2007), which appeared to correspond with these four competences. Although project type and characteristics are acknowledged as perhaps placing more emphasis on some competences over others, the competences identified within the framework are suggested as having a broad application. The competency framework categorizes two groups of competences as those pertaining to performance and personal dimensions. Personal competences are those identified as capturing the specific sets of skills to "enable effective interaction with others" (PMI, 2008, p. 23). These are further arranged into six unit areas (communicating, leading, managing, cognitive ability, effectiveness, and professionalism), containing 25 elements overall.

The first stage involved selecting items for inclusion in each of the four competence areas from the complete range of behaviors identified in the framework, which on face content appeared to be associated with the four project manager competences that are the focus of the study. This resulted in 24 project management behaviors that were grouped into the four project manager competence domains. These are shown in Table 3 mapped against the specific PMI competence elements listed in the PMI framework. Face validity of these items was then further investigated with a small group of six project managers not participating in the research. This resulted in all 24 items being retained for each of the competences as follows: communication (4 items), teamwork (7 items), attentiveness (5 items) and managing conflict (8 items).

All 24 items were then organized into an instrument that formed a part of a larger questionnaire which participants completed online. Participants responses were then subject to an exploratory factor analysis using principal components with a varimax rotation. The rotation converged in 15 iterations resulting in a six-factor solution, accounting for 36.4%, 9.6%, 7.5%, 5.6%, 4.6%, and 4.5% of the variance, all with Eigen values greater than 1. The factor loadings are presented in Table 4. Items were retained for factors where weights were greater than 0.40, where there was no cross loading, and where items appeared to be theoretically consistent. Nearly all items retained on scales were consistent with those initially identified through face validity. The major exceptions were from the teamwork scale, where only one item was retained from those initially posited and two further items were drawn from the attentiveness and managing conflict behavioral domains. These three items were determined to have theoretical integrity when compared to the

Table 3. Grouping PMI Project Management Competence Elements into Key Project Management Competence Measures

Project Manager Competences	PMCD Framework Element
Communication	
1. Understood the communication from others involved in the project?	6.1
2. Maintained formal communication channels?	6.2
3. Maintained informal communication channels?	6.2
4. Communicated appropriately with different audiences?	6.4
Teamwork	
5. Encouraged teamwork consistently?	8.1
6. Shared your knowledge and expertise with others involved in on the project?	8.1
7. Maintained good working relationships with others involved on the project?	8.1
8. Worked with others to clearly identify project scope, roles, expectations, and tasks specifications?	8.2
9. Built trust an,d confidence with both stakeholders and others involved on the project?	11.4
10. Helped to create an environment of openness and consideration on the project?	11.4
11. Helped to create an environment of confidence and respect for individual differences?	11.4
Attentiveness	
12. Responded to and acted upon expectations, concerns and issues raised by others in the project?	6.1
13. Actively listened to other project team members or stakeholders involved in the project?	6.1
14. Expressed positive expectations of others involved on the project?	7.3
15. Helped to build a positive attitude and optimism for success on the project?	7.3
16. Engaged stakeholders involved in the project?	10.2
Managing Conflict	
17. Helped others to see different points of view or perspectives?	8.3
18. Recognized conflict?	8.3
19. Resolved conflict?	8.3
20. Worked effectively with the organizational politics associated with the project?	9.1
21. Helped to solve relationship issues and problems that emerged on the project?	10.1
22. Attempted to build consensus in the best interests of the project?	10.2
23. Managed ambiguous situations satisfactorily while supporting the project's goals?	10.3
24. Maintained self-control and responded calmly and appropriately in all situations?	11.3

Table 4. Varimax-Rotated Loadings on a Six-Factor Solution of Project Manager Competences ($N = 67$)

Competence	Factor 1 Managing Conflict	Factor 2 Communication	Factor 3 Teamwork	Factor 4 Attentiveness	Factor 5	Factor 6
Comm1	−0.01	**0.57**	0.03	0.30	0.25	−0.31
Comm2	0.03	−0.02	0.14	0.87	−0.16	−0.03
Comm3	0.11	**0.58**	0.16	0.26	0.27	0.09
Comm4	0.16	**0.58**	0.14	0.33	0.17	0.07
Team5	0.37	−0.04	**0.75**	0.14	0.02	0.04
Team6	0.77	0.16	0.20	0.08	−0.02	−0.06
Team7	0.14	0.38	0.12	0.45	0.42	−0.13
Team8	0.00	0.12	0.48	0.45	0.32	0.16
Team9	0.28	0.49	0.20	0.36	0.20	0.00
Team10	0.35	0.02	0.44	0.29	0.48	0.16
Team11	0.30	0.26	0.23	−0.08	**0.72**	0.16
Atten12	0.28	0.17	0.38	**0.49**	0.10	−0.33
Atten13	0.14	0.37	0.20	**0.52**	0.13	−0.43
Atten14	0.04	0.61	0.57	0.05	0.21	0.02
Atten15	0.15	0.22	**0.66**	0.14	0.17	0.36
Atten16	0.10	0.16	0.04	**0.70**	0.08	0.18
Conflict17	0.38	0.20	**0.74**	0.13	0.16	−0.17
Conflict18	0.41	0.67	−0.21	−0.01	−0.09	0.20
Conflict19	**0.77**	0.17	0.14	0.10	0.16	-0.02
Conflict20	0.16	0.12	0.21	0.16	0.22	**0.72**
Conflict21	**0.73**	0.22	0.11	0.16	0.37	0.18
Conflcit22	**0.65**	0.26	0.12	0.14	0.41	0.04
Conflict23	**0.69**	0.07	0.33	-0.03	0.16	0.14
Conflict24	0.19	0.09	0.09	0.04	**0.82**	0.02

literature relating to effective teamwork behaviors, and so they were retained (Cohen & Bailey, 1997; Marks, Mathieu, & Zaccaro, 2001; Rickards, Chen, & Moger, 2001; Salas, Sims, & Burke, 2005).

3.4.3.1 *Data Analyses*

All statistical analyses were conducted using SPSS 15. Initial tests began by performing bivariate correlations in order to explore initial relationships between variables measured in the study. This was then followed by conducting a series of regression analyses where each of the four project manager competences was regressed in turn against emotional intelligence measures and empathy. The next set of analyses followed the same procedure, but instead regressed each of the four dimensions of transformational leadership. Both investigations were undertaken by entering IQ, personality measures, and certification as control variables in the first step, followed by the four EI branch scores, total EI score, and empathy in the second step.

3.5 Results

Correlational analyses were used as an initial examination of relationships between the variables studied. Table 5 summarizes the means, standard deviations, and inter-correlations among all the variables used in the study. Total EI was significantly correlated with all four of its constituent branches: perceiving emotions ($r = 0.82$, $p < 0.01$), using emotions to facilitate thinking ($r = 0.81$, $p < 0.01$), understanding emotions ($r = 0.52$, $p < 0.01$), and managing emotions ($r = 0.59$, $p < 0.01$). The significant correlations found were as expected, if these individual branches are part of a much wider overall construct of emotional intelligence. A number of significant correlations were found between EI measures and the dependent measures examined in the study. Branch 2, using emotions to facilitate thinking, Branch 3, understanding emotions, and the overall EI score were all found to positively correlate with the project manager competence of managing conflict ($r = 0.27$, $p < 0.05$), ($r = 0.31$, $p < 0.05$), and ($r = 0.30$, $p < 0.05$), respectively. Both of the abilities, using emotions and understanding emotions, also positively correlated with the project manager competence of teamwork ($r = 0.29$, $p < 0.05$) and ($r = 0.31$, $p < 0.05$). Using emotions to facilitate thinking was the only EI ability found to have any significant correlation with transformational leadership and this was in relation to the two dimensions of idealized influence ($r = 0.26$, $p < 0.05$) and individualized consideration ($r = 0.27$, $p < 0.05$). Both total EI and branch scores showed minor correlations with personality, offering further support for the predominantly independent nature of these two aspects of individual difference. Only three positive correlations were found and these were between conscientiousness and managing emotions ($r = 0.33$, $p < 0.05$), and agreeableness with using emotions to facilitate thinking ($r = 0.33$, $p < 0.01$) and the overall EI score ($r = 0.25$, $p < 0.05$). Previously, agreeableness, emotional stability, and extraversion were found to be related to dimensions of EI (Day & Carroll, 2004; Lopes, Salovey, & Strauss, 2003). A positive relationship to agreeableness is often found given that this scale is often seen as reflecting compassion and cooperation. The positive relationship with conscientiousness is possibly explained given that conscientiousness is often thought to capture aspects of personality associated with self-discipline rather than acting spontaneously (Hogan & Ones, 1997). These are behaviors closely associated with impulse control, and this forms a key part of managing one's own emotions.

Both using emotions to facilitate thinking ($r = 0.24$, $p < 0.05$), and total EI ($r = 0.28$, $p < 0.05$), were found to be positively correlated with empathy. Given that empathy involves having to think about emotions in order to respond empathically, these results are consistent with a number of other previous studies showing that ability EI measures can correlate with self-judgments of empathetic feeling (Brackett, Rivers, Shiffman, Lerner, & Salovey, 2006; Caruso, Mayer, & Salovey, 2002; Ciarrochi, Chan, & Caputi, 2000). Significant positive correlations were also found between empathy and the personality dimension of agreeableness ($r = 0.59$, $p < 0.01$) and between empathy and the project manager competence of attentiveness ($r = 0.28$, $p < 0.05$). This again appears to support previous findings in the literature that show a significant relationship between empathy and displaying considerate or prosocial behaviors (Eisenberg & Miller, 1987). The significant negative correlation between empathy and the transformational leadership dimension of intellectual stimulation ($r = -0.25$, $p < 0.05$) was unexpected and seemed counter-intuitive to the prevailing view that transformational leadership is based upon a strong emotional relationship between leaders and followers. There was also a negative correlation obtained between empathy and emotional stability ($r = 0.28$, $p < 0.05$). Both of these findings may be due to the empathy measure used here, capturing emotional rather than cognitive dimensions of empathy with a particular emphasis on elements relating to individual's emotional responses to others in distress. Previously, this aspect of empathy was found to be negatively associated with transformational leadership (Skinner & Spurgeon, 2005).

It should also be noted that that there were a number of positive correlations found between personality measures and the project manager competence of managing conflict: extraversion ($r = 0.26$, $p < 0.05$), emotional stability ($r = 0.36$, $p < 0.01$), and openness ($r = 0.43$, $p < 0.01$). Openness was also found to positively correlate with the project manager competence of teamwork ($r = 0.28$, $p < 0.05$). In addition, personality measures accounted for the largest number of both high and significant correlations with transformational leadership dimensions here. Extraversion correlated with influence ($r = 0.385$, $p < 0.01$), motivation ($r = 0.29$, $p < 0.05$) and stimulation ($r = 0.34$, $p < 0.01$). Emotional stability correlated with influence ($r = 0.25$, $p < 0.05$) and stimulation ($r = 0.44$, $p < 0.01$). Openness correlated with motivation ($r = 0.46$, $p < 0.01$), stimulation ($r = 0.51$, $p < 0.01$), and consideration ($r = 0.46$, $p < 0.01$). Four of the five personality dimensions were found to have positive and significant correlations with the overall transformational leadership scale: extraversion ($r = 0.39$, $p < 0.01$), agreeableness ($r = 0.27$, $p < 0.05$), emotional stability ($r = 0.33$, $p < 0.01$), and openness ($r = 0.52$, $p < 0.01$). Finally, it is worth commenting that cognitive ability was found to correlate positively with the project manager competence of teamwork ($r = 0.26$, $p < 0.05$) but not with any of the remaining

Table 5. Intercorrelations Between All Variables in Study One

Variables	Mean (SD)	1	2	3	4	5	6
1. GMA	118.85 (9.55)						
2. Extraversion	33.54 (7.47)	−0.10					
3. Agreeableness	41.03 (5.08)	−0.07	0.23				
4. Conscientiousness	36.97 (6.09)	−0.14	−0.08	0.12			
5. Emotional stability	33.78 (7.15)	0.40**	0.04	−0.09	0.07		
6. Openness	30.87 (4.50)	0.05	0.17	0.32**	−0.03	−0.02	
7. Perceiving emotions	94.54 (17.72)	−0.05	−0.07	0.14	0.24	−0.00	−0.02
8. Using emotions	95.52 (14.88)	0.06	0.03	0.33**	0.06	−0.03	0.11
9. Understand emotions	98.05 (8.85)	0.24	−0.08	0.01	0.01	0.12	0.11
10. Manage emotions	94.48 (7.48)	0.12	−0.04	0.21	0.33**	0.09	0.09
11. Total EI	94.52 (12.49)	0.09	-0.07	0.25*	0.24	0.03	0.06
12. Empathy	31.33 (22.15)	−0.07	0.10	0.59**	0.05	−0.28*	0.00
13. Teamwork	5.43 (.82)	0.26*	0.23	0.16	0.17	0.27*	0.28*
14. Communication	5.55 (.68)	0.07	0.04	0.22	0.12	0.18	0.12
15. Attentiveness	5.59 (.65)	−0.07	0.10	0.20	0.20	0.13	0.13
16. Managing conflict	5.30 (.78)	0.13	0.26*	0.23	0.11	0.36**	0.43**
17. Influence	2.79 (.48)	0.06	0.38**	0.24	0.23	0.25*	0.20
18. Motivation	2.55 (.54)	0.12	0.29*	0.30*	0.11	0.20	0.46**
19. Stimulation	2.40 (.71)	0.17	0.34**	0.08	0.02	0.44**	0.51**
20. Consideration	2.80 (.59)	−0.02	0.24	0.29*	0.25*	0.12	0.46**
21. Transformational		0.11	0.39**	0.27*	0.18	0.33**	0.52**

Variable	17	18	19	20
18. Motivation	0.55**			
19. Stimulation	0.37**	0.65**		
20. Consideration	0.47**	0.54**	0.53**	
21. Transformational	0.71**	0.85**	0.83**	0.80**

7	8	9	10	11	12	13	14	15	16
0.51**									
0.22	0.42**								
0.28*	0.42**	0.14							
0.82**	0.81**	0.52**	0.59**						
0.16	0.24*	0.21	0.21	0.28*					
0.08	0.29*	0.31*	0.14	0.25*	0.10				
0.13	0.21	0.11	0.08	0.18	0.20	0.36**			
0.07	0.21	0.16	0.09	0.17	0.28*	0.46**	0.61**		
0.16	0.27*	0.31*	0.21	0.30*	−0.04	0.58**	0.41**	0.40**	
0.16	0.26*	0.12	0.19	0.23	0.07	0.46**	0.33**	0.27*	0.49**
−0.02	0.08	0.11	0.13	0.07	0.07	0.59**	0.26*	0.28*	0.53**
−0.07	−0.04	−0.03	0.17	−0.02	−0.25*	0.46**	−0.03	0.05	0.53**
0.05	0.27*	0.05	0.19	0.16	−0.06	0.42**	0.07	0.17	0.45**
0.03	0.16	0.07	0.21	0.12	−0.07	0.60**	0.17	0.22	0.62**

competences, nor with any transformational leadership measures. This may suggest that both personality and aspects of EI have far more salience in underpinning these particular competences and leadership behaviors than cognitive ability.

Results of the first set of hierarchical regressions are shown in Table 6. The emotional intelligence ability, understanding emotions, was found to be significantly associated with the project manager competence of teamwork ($\beta = 0.28$, $p < 0.05$, $\Delta R^2 = 0.07$). The two personality dimensions of openness and emotional stability together accounted for 13% of the variation for this competence, with this EI ability explaining a further 7%. Partial support was therefore found for hypothesis 1. None of the relationships with EI measures or empathy with the project manager competence of communication were found to be significant ($F [6,61] = 0.85$, $p > n.s.$), providing no support for hypothesis 2. Empathy was found to be significantly associated with the project manager competence of attentiveness ($\beta = 0.28$, $p < 0.05$). However, no significant relationships were found between this project manager competence and any of the EI measures. Partial support was therefore found for hypothesis 3. Of note, neither cognitive ability nor personality was found to be associated with this competence, with empathy solely accounting for a 7% variation in this competence.

The overall EI score was also found to be significantly associated with the project manager competence, managing conflict ($\beta = 0.26$, $p < 0.01$, $\Delta R^2 = 0.06$). Again both the personality dimensions of emotional stability and openness were found to account for most variation in the project manager competence, jointly accounting for a significant 30% with the overall EI score explaining the additional 6%. Partial support was therefore found for hypothesis 4. Finally, the emotional ability, using emotions to facilitate thinking was found to be significantly associated with the transformational leadership dimensions of idealized influence ($\beta = 0.23$, $p < 0.05$, $\Delta R^2 = 0.04$) and individualized consideration ($\beta = 0.26$, $p < 0.01$, $\Delta R^2 = 0.06$).

Significantly, the personality dimensions of emotional stability ($\beta = 0.31$, $p < 0.01$, $\Delta R^2 = 0.08$), and openness ($\beta = 0.26$, $p < 0.05$, $\Delta R^2 = 0.06$) were also both found to be positively associated with teamwork and similarly with managing conflict (emotional stability [$\beta = 0.27$, $p < 0.05$, $\Delta R^2 = 0.15$]; openness [$\beta = 0.38$, $p < 0.01$, $\Delta R^2 = 0.08$]). Openness was also significantly related to the project management competence of attentiveness ($\beta = 0.79$, $p < 0.05$, $\Delta R^2 = 0.04$), explaining an additional 4% variation. Partial support was therefore found for hypothesis 5.

In addition it should be noted that personality attributes were found to be significantly associated with all four transformational leadership dimensions. Both extraversion ($\beta = 0.39$, $p < 0.01$, $\Delta R^2 = 0.13$) and conscientiousness ($\beta = 0.25$, $p < 0.05$, $\Delta R^2 = 0.06$) were significantly associated with idealized influence. Extraversion ($\beta = 0.22$, $p < 0.05$, $\Delta R^2 = 0.03$) and openness ($\beta = 0.42$, $p < 0.001$, $\Delta R^2 = 0.20$) were strongly associated with inspirational motivation. Openness ($\beta = 0.48$, $p < 0.000$, $\Delta R^2 = 0.24$), emotional stability ($\beta = 0.44$, $p < 0.000$, $\Delta R^2 = 0.20$), and extraversion ($\beta = 0.24$, $p < 0.01$, $\Delta R^2 = 0.04$) were strongly associated with intellectual stimulation. Openness ($\beta = 0.47$, $p < 0.01$, $\Delta R^2 = 0.20$) and conscientiousness ($\beta = 0.27$, $p < 0.05$, $\Delta R^2 = 0.06$) were both significantly associated with individualized consideration.

Table 6. Results of Hierarchical Regression Analysis of Project Competences (*N* = 67)

	Teamwork				Communication				Attentiveness				Managing Conflict			
	β	R^2	ΔR^2	*F*	β	R^2	ΔR^2	*F*	β	R^2	ΔR^2	*F*	β	R^2	ΔR^2	*F*
Step 1																
Certification	0.01	**0.13**	**0.05**		0.00				-0.12				0.22	**0.30**	**0.12**	
GMA	0.24	**0.07**	**0.07**		0.08				0.06				-0.06	**0.18**	**0.18**	
Extraversion	0.16				0.00				0.08				0.21			
Conscientiousnss	0.18				0.14				0.18				0.07			
Agreeableness	0.08				0.12				0.05				0.16			
Emotional stability	**0.29***				0.26				0.23				**0.37***			
Openness	**0.26***				0.10				0.23				**0.43****			
Step 2																
Perceiving (B1)	-0.07	**0.20**	**0.07**	**6.33****	0.42			0.85 n.s.	0.03	**0.07**		**5.62***	-0.14	**0.36**	**0.06**	**13.41****
Using (B2)	**0.28***				0.43				0.16				0.09			
Understand (B3)	0.16				0.17				0.10				0.12			
Manage (B4)	-0.03				0.16				0.04				-0.02			
Total EI	-0.01				-0.75				0.10				**0.26****			
Empathy	0.13				0.17				**0.28***				-0.02			

Note: Standardized regression coefficients are from the full model. R^2 is adjusted.
* $p<0.05$, ** $p<0.01$; *** $p<0.001$.

Four out of the five measures of personality were found to be associated with the overall transformational leadership scale: openness ($\beta = 0.48$, $p < 0.01$, $\Delta R^2 = 0.26$), emotional stability ($\beta = 0.31$, $p < 0.01$, $\Delta R^2 = 0.10$), extraversion ($\beta = .31$, $p < 0.01$, $\Delta R^2 = 0.08$), and conscientiousness ($\beta = 0.20$, $p < 0.05$, $\Delta R^2 = 0.03$). Together personality characteristics were found to account for 26% variation in the measure of overall transformational leadership behavior.

3.6 Discussion

The results from this study take forward our understanding of the role that emotional intelligence may play in projects in two major ways. The first concerns the demonstration of relationships between aspects of the individual differences associated with emotional intelligence and project manager competences that have been suggested to be important for successful outcomes in projects. Both the emotional intelligence ability, *using emotions to facilitate thinking,* and an overall measure of EI ability were found to be associated with the project manager competences of teamwork and managing conflict, respectively. Previously Druskat and Druskat (2006) have suggested that competences in these two areas are especially important for successful project outcomes due to the specific nature of projects. More significantly, they suggested that emotional intelligence is likely to underpin behaviors associated with these competences. This study is the first to offer some empirical support for this proposition. Of importance, both of these areas of emotional intelligence were found to provide additional explanatory power in these competences after controlling for both cognitive ability and personality, with the ability, using emotions to facilitate thinking, and overall EI ability accounting for an additional 7% and 6% variation in teamwork and managing conflict competences, respectively.

These findings are also in broad support of previous findings in the literature that have found significant relationships using ability conceptualizations of emotional intelligence and the use of better conflict management strategies (Jordan & Troth, 2004) as well as the few studies that have investigated their relationships with key behaviors associated with teamwork (Clarke, forthcoming; Ilarda & Findlay, 2006). Ilarda and Findlay (2006), for example, conducted a study of 134 individuals working in teams across a range of industrial sectors and found that emotional intelligence was significantly associated with a propensity for teamwork. More recently, Clarke (forthcoming), found significant relationships between the two emotional intelligence abilities, using emotions to facilitate thinking and managing emotions, and interpersonal team behaviors (associated with managing conflict and promoting positive affect) in a student population. Importantly, that study also found no significant relationship between these interpersonal team behaviors and cognitive ability as measured by a student's grade point average scores. The finding obtained from this current study, that cognitive ability was not associated with either of these two project manager competences, would therefore seem to offer some support for the view that cognitive ability plays a far more limited role in these particular relationship management behaviors.

The study also found a significant positive relationship between empathy and the project manager competence of attentiveness. This competence captures key behaviors associated with: engaging with project members in order to build strong relationships, responding to their concerns, and building positive attitudes for project success. The significance of empathy for developing close interpersonal bonds and supportive relationships has been recognized in the psychology literature for some time (Gladstein, 1983; Goldstein & Michaels, 1985; Rogers, 1975). More recently, it has also been linked to effective leader behaviors, such as showing consideration and attentiveness to the needs of followers (House & Podsakoff, 1994; Yukl, 1998). A number of authors have suggested that emotional abilities, such as perceiving and understanding emotions in others, may underpin empathy (Ashkanasy & Tse, 2000; Cooper & Sawaf, 1997). It may well be that the failure to find any significant relationships between emotional intelligence abilities and this project manager competence is due to the fact that they are mediated by empathy. The failure to find any significant relationships between personality and attentiveness was surprising since openness and agreeableness might be expected to be associated with showing considerate and attentive behaviors. Both of these personality dimensions have also been shown to be moderately related to empathy (Davies, Stankov, & Roberts, 1998). It is possible that the relatively small sample in the study placed constraints on the statistical tests used, thereby accounting for the failure to determine any effects.

This could similarly explain the failure to find any significant relationships between any of the independent and control variables and the project manager competence of communication. The measure used was found to have good reliability ($\alpha = 0.70$) and captured behaviors associated with both informal communication and understanding communication from others involved in the project. Emotional intelligence abilities are believed to be associated with more effective communication through emotional expressivity and in recognizing the emotional content of others' communication (emotional sensitivity) (Morand, 2001; Riggio & Reichard, 2008). Communication has been identified as a chief factor associated with successful outcomes in projects (Kerzner, 2001; Lester, 1998; Munns & Bjerimi, 1996) associated with a wide range of project manager behaviors. These extend far beyond face-to-face communication and involve a myriad of communication modes available. It may be that the measure of project manager competence utilized here is far too broad in its domain to sufficiently capture the type of communication more likely to be associated with either emotional intelligence or empathy. Previous research of relationships between personality and nonverbal forms of communication has also been mixed (Cunningham & Elmhurst, 1977; Gillford, 2006), which could also explain the failure to find any relationships in relation to the personality measures here.

The second major contribution of the study is that this is the first study to show a relationship between emotional intelligence abilities and transformational leadership, after controlling for both cognitive ability and personality. Whereas a number of studies have previously found a significant relationship between EI and transformational leadership (e.g,. Barling, Slater, & Kelloway, 2000; Butler &

Table 7. Results of Hierarchical Regression Analysis of Transformational Leadership ($N = 67$)

	Idealized Influence				Inspirational Motivation			
	β	R^2	ΔR^2	F	β	R^2	ΔR^2	F
Step 1								
Certification	0.02				−0.03			
GMA	0.09				0.12			
Extraversion	0.39**	0.13	0.13		0.22*	0.23	0.03	
Conscientiousnss	0.25*	0.19	0.06		0.14			
Agreeableness	0.05				0.14			
Emotional Stability	0.22				0.19			
Openness	0.12				0.42***	0.20	0.20	11.03***
Step 2								
Perceiving (B1)	0.02				0.01			
Using (B2)	0.23*	0.23	0.04	7.62***	0.04			
Understand (B3)	0.06				0.08			
Manage (B4)	0.03				0.10			
Total EI	0.04				0.06			
Empathy	−0.04				0.05			

Note: Standardized regression coefficients are from the full model. R^2 is adjusted.
*$p<0.05$, **$p<0.01$; ***$p<0.001$.

Chinowsky, 2006; Mandell & Pherwani, 2003; Sivananthan & Fekken, 2002) most of these have used mixed model measures of EI that have been criticized for sharing a considerable degree of overlap with existing personality measures (Brackett & Mayer, 2003; Dawda & Hart, 2000). To date, only four studies have appeared in the literature that have used an ability-derived measure of emotional intelligence to examine relationships with leadership (Downey, Papageorgiou, & Stough, 2005; Kerr, Garvin, Heaton, & Boyle, 2006; Leban & Zulauf, 2004; Rosete & Ciarrochi, 2005). Of these, only the study by Leban & Zulauf (2004) examined the relationship with emotional intelligence and transformational leadership measures and this was in a project management context. They found a significant relationship between participants' overall EI score and the transformational leadership dimension of inspirational motivation. Again, a limitation with the study was the failure to control for both cognitive ability and personality. This is problematic since a wide range of personal characteristics have previously been found to be associated with transformational leadership (Atwater & Yammarino, 1993; Bommer, Rubin, & Baldwin, 2004; Bono & Judge, 2004).

Indeed, significant relationships were also found between personality measures and transformational leadership. Extraversion and conscientiousness were associated with the dimension of idealized influence. Extraversion and openness were associated with the dimension of inspirational motivation. Extraversion, emotional stability, and openness were associated with intellectual

Intellectual Stimulation				Individualized Consideration				Transformational Leadership			
β	R²	ΔR²	F	β	R²	ΔR²	F	β	R²	ΔR²	F
0.05				0.03				0.03			
−0.01				−0.04				−0.01			
0.24**	0.48	0.04		0.18				0.31**	0.44	0.08	
0.02				0.27*	0.26	0.06		0.20*	0.47	0.03	15.71**
−0.10				0.12				0.06			
0.44***	0.44	0.20		0.11				0.31**	0.36	0.10	
0.48***	0.24	0.24	21.69***	0.47**	0.20	0.20		0.48**	0.26	0.26	
−0.05				0.51				0.01			
−0.09				0.79*		0.04	4.50**	0.10			
−0.12				0.19				0.00			
0.09				0.30				0.09			
−0.05				−1.24				0.06			
−0.17				−0.10	0.30			−0.03			

stimulation. Finally, conscientiousness and openness were associated with the fourth dimension of individualized consideration. It is important to note that the emotional ability, using emotions to facilitate thinking, was found to account for a further 4% in variation of both the transformational leadership dimensions of idealized influence and individualized consideration after first controlling for personality.

This is the first study then that has shown the additional predictive power of emotional intelligence *abilities* to account for variations in these transformational leadership dimensions after personality. Rosete and Ciarrochi (2005) also found the emotional ability, perceiving emotions, to account for an additional variation of 10% in leadership scores after controlling for personality (using the 16PF). However, this was based on performance management ratings of leadership and not specifically transformational leadership behaviors. The ability to use emotions to facilitate thinking may be important in order to foster high-quality, interpersonal relationships between leaders and followers (Graen & Uhl-Bien, 1995). This ability should enable the project manager to better discern the emotional climate among other project members, and then assist them in thinking how best to respond to their needs and concerns, for example, through promoting more positive feelings of optimism and excitement after a setback. This capacity for promoting positive affect is seen as a key element associated with building trust (Jones & George, 1998). The transformational leadership behavior dimensions of both individualized consideration and idealized influence would seem to be closely associated with both of these areas (Bass, Avolio, Jung, & Berson, 2003; Gardner & Avolio, 1998). The finding here that the emotional ability, *Using Emotions to Facilitate Thinking*, accounts for incremental variation in these transformational leadership behaviors after personality, is therefore significant.

3.7 Conclusions

To date, only five studies have appeared in the literature investigating the concept of emotional intelligence specifically within the context of projects. In these studies, emotional intelligence has been suggested as particularly important in projects due to the nature of this form of work organization. This places specific emphasis on project manager behaviors associated with communication, teamwork, attentiveness, and managing conflict as being important to successful project outcomes. This is the first study to use the ability measure of EI and examine its relationship with specific behaviors that are associated with project manager competence in these areas. Both the emotional intelligence ability, using emotions to facilitate thinking, and the participants' overall EI scores were found to be significantly associated with the competences of teamwork and managing conflict, respectively. Project managers' empathy was also found to be significantly associated with the competence of attentiveness. In addition, the emotional intelligence ability was also found to be significantly associated with the transformational leadership dimensions of idealized influence and individualized consideration. In each instance, these EI dimensions were found to offer additional predictive capacity in both the competence and leadership behavioral domains after controlling for both cognitive ability and personality.

The results suggest that emotional intelligence abilities and empathy offer a means to further explain aspects of individual differences between project managers that can influence their performance in projects. However, the results need to be interpreted within the limitations associated with the study. The most significant concern is the approach used to measure both project manager competences and transformational leadership behaviors. This relied on self-report ratings from those taking part in the study. Subjective self-ratings of performance have consistently been found to be more lenient than those provided by observers (Atwater & Yammarino, 1992; Carless, Mann, & Wearing, 1998; Mabe & West, 1982) and a number of authors have urged caution in relying upon such measures within organizational research (Schmidt & Hunter, 1998; Spector, 1994). This has often resulted in researchers using peer report measures, believing these offer improved validity in performance measures. However, recent research suggests that the picture is somewhat more complicated. Recent research by Atkins and Wood (2002) comparing self, peer, and supervisor ratings of performance with objective measures of performance in an assessment center found that peer and supervisor ratings of performance were not always predictive of objective performance measures. In particular, the highest peer ratings were found to be associated with poor performance. Higher self- and peer ratings were also predictive of higher supervisor ratings. However, when compared to the objective measure of performance, both the supervisors and peers overestimated performance. Instead, highest performance was associated with low self-scores and modest peer scores. It is not all clear that using aggregated peer measures of either project manager competence or transformational leadership behavior would necessarily have given more valid performance scores than those of self-ratings. Nonetheless, the constraints imposed in conducting a pilot study precluded the use of more objective performance measures which suggest the findings should be treated as only suggestive at this stage.

A further major limitation of the study is again the problems of validity due to common method variance (Spector, 1987). However, following recommendations by Podsakoff, Mackenzie, Podsakoff, and Lee (2003), a number of procedural strategies were used to attempt to minimize these effects. The first of these related to a proximal separation of measures. Measures were obtained from participants who completed two tests and one questionnaire. The two tests measured EI and cognitive ability, and presented items in a different format to the questionnaire. In addition, where scales were used to assess differing measures, these varied in length including 5, 7, and 9-point scales. A psychological separation was also made between these measures in that individuals had to log into three different websites each with their own pass codes in order to complete each measure. Instructions given to respondents were to complete each of the instruments at different sittings over the 2- week data collection period, thereby also providing a temporal separation between measures. Assurances of confidentiality were also made in order to reduce problems associated with social desirability in answering. It should also be borne in mind that the study only used cross-sectional data to analyze relationships between emotional intelligence and dependent measures, thus precluding any definitive statements relating to causality.

The final set of limitations relates to both the measures used and the sample. Relatively low reliabilities were found for a number of scales used in the study. A reliability coefficient of only 0.55 was obtained for the managing emotions ability branch of EI. This is lower than has been reported in previous studies and suggests that there were problems encountered here with the validity of this measure. Previously Clarke (2006a) raised concerns specifically regarding the use of a test to satisfactorily capture an ability, such as managing emotions, where strategies used are so varied and dependent on context. This may represent a wider problem with the measure itself or may be related to the particular sample. The low reliability may then have accounted for the failure to detect and significant relationships with this particular branch of EI. In addition, the two measures of transformational leadership dimensions representing inspirational motivation and individualized consideration similarly were found to have low reliabilities of 0.52 and 0.55, respectively. The use of self-report measures may well account for these low reliabilities. However, it does suggest that the significant relationship found between the emotional ability, using emotions to facilitate thinking, and individualized consideration should be treated with some degree of caution. It should also be noted that no significant correlations were found between general mental ability and any of the emotional intelligence measures used in the study. Previous researchers have reported significant moderate correlations between intelligence and EI ability measures (Lopes, Salovey, & Strauss, 2003) and Rode et al. (2007) reported a correlation of $r = 0.20$, $p < 0.01$ between GMA and the total EI ability score using the same GMA measure used herein. The failure to find any significant relationships, therefore, raises some concern. One potential explanation could lie with the measure of IQ used in the study. A number of participants in the study indicated that they had problems with the American English used on the test, particularly in the verbal reasoning domains which they believed impeded their performance in this time-constrained test. This may suggest that the general ability scores obtained are subject to some bias and may not reflect accurate measures of ability.

In addition, the relatively modest sample size of 67 is also a limitation here. This may have increased the risk of statistical Type I errors where results are found to be significant. Finally, some further mention should be made of the population upon which this study is based. These were drawn from two organizations involved in arts, education, research and development, and construction, as well as a small number from the UK Chapter of the Project Management Institute who are predominantly involved in consultancy and professional services. This arguably represents a far more diverse project management base than had been traditionally studied. In addition, just over a quarter of these (27%) were certified in project management. The extent to which the results found here are able to be generalized beyond this particular sample to project managers more widely operating in traditional project management industries and sectors is therefore unknown.

Section 4.0

An Evaluation of the Impact of Emotional Intelligence Training

4.1 Introduction

With increasing evidence suggesting that emotional intelligence (EI) is able to predict a wide range of key behaviors associated with effectively working in and managing projects (Butler & Chinowski, 2006; Leban & Zulauf, 2004; Muller & Turner, 2007), the question of whether emotional intelligence can be developed is becoming of far greater interest to the project management community. The expectation is that, by developing the emotional intelligence of those working in projects, gains should eventually be seen in terms of improvements in those project management behaviors deemed important to successful projects (Turner & Lloyd-Walker, 2008). Determining whether emotional intelligence can be improved through training and development interventions for project managers is therefore an important first step. However, building a significant body of knowledge to underpin training interventions in this area presents a number of significant challenges. In a recent review of emotional intelligence training, Clarke (2006b) concluded that there was minimal evidence available to support many of the claims that EI training was effective. Furthermore, the use of differing EI models to underpin training, alongside the disparate measures used to evaluate its impact, meant that the literature was both fragmented and lacking in coherence. Making comparisons across studies to identify factors associated with the design of training that might be associated with its effectiveness is therefore also difficult.

From a developmental perspective, how emotional intelligence is characterized, either as a set of dispositions or personality attributes (Bar-On, 1997; Dulewicz & Higgs, 2003), cognitive abilities associated with the processing of emotional information (Mayer & Salovey, 1997), or a taxonomy of competences (Boyzatis, Goleman, & Rhee, 2000), clearly has considerable implications for designing the content and delivery of any developmental intervention. The use of these differing models to underpin training interventions also raises far more complex questions as to whether emotional intelligence as defined by these differing perspectives can actually be developed at all. For example, those dimensions of emotional intelligence models that seem to share greater resemblance to aspects of personality may be far less amenable to change through training, given that personality is widely recognized as a set of relatively stable patterns of characteristics and dispositions (Donnelian, Conger, & Burzette, 2007; Gross, 1987; Rantanen, Metsapelto, Feldt, Pulkkinen, & Kokko, 2007). In addition, despite accumulating research which suggests that the ability model of EI may have greater construct validity, relatively few studies have been published that have specifically investigated the impact of training interventions using this model.

It is within this context that this study makes a contribution to the literature by presenting findings from an evaluation of an emotional intelligence training program that was designed to target a number of participants' emotional intelligence abilities. The results show some positive effects for training. Beyond identifying training impact, the study also advances theory building in this area by identifying factors associated with the design of training that appear associated with the development of EI ability. Finally, the study makes a contribution more specifically to the project management field, by examining the effects of training on a sample of project managers in the UK, and identifying whether changes also occur in their self-assessed project management competences. The findings are therefore of particular significance for those considering how best to design development strategies to enhance project management performance with emotional intelligence as a key focus.

4.2 Findings From Emotional Intelligence Development Studies to Date

A search of the literature located seven studies that reported evaluations of interventions designed to develop emotional intelligence (Table 8). Two of these studies used competence based measures of emotional intelligence drawn from Goleman's Emotional Competence Inventory (Sala, 2006; Turner & Lloyd-Walker, 2008). Sala (2006) reported the results of two training programs, one involving 20 managers and consultants and the other involving 19 participants from a U.S. accounting organization, collecting postcourse measures at 8 and 14 months, respectively, for the two groups. Positive effects were reported for the training on 8 of the 20 emotional intelligence competence areas examined. Turner and Lloyd-Walker (2008) evaluated the impact of a training program on 42 project management employees based in a U.S. defense project. Emotional intelligence was assessed through self- and peer ratings using Goleman's (1998) Emotional Competence Inventory (Boyatzis, Goleman, & Rhee, 2000). Measures of job satisfaction and job performance were also collected with all postcourse measures collected 6 months following training. Generally they concluded positive effects for the training intervention in terms of self-ECI ratings but no effects for peer ratings of ECI competences. The picture was somewhat more complex, in that most of the positive

Table 8. Emotional Intelligence Training/Development Evaluation Studies

Authors	EI measure	Research Design	Intervention	Results
Slaski & Cartwright (2003)	1. EQ-i (Bar-On 1997) 2. EIQ (Dulewicz & Higgs 2000)	Pre/post-test (6 months)	60 retail managers attended 4-day training program over 4 weeks	1. Positive changes in all but one of the EQ-i subscales 2. Mixed results on the EQ-I subscales
Moriarty & Buckley (2003)	WEIP-5 (Jordan et al. 2002)	Pre/post-test	80 UG students attended a 12-week teamwork program	Mixed results: 1. Self-assessed ability to deal with others' emotions 2. Peer-assessed ability to deal with own and others' emotions
Meyer, Fletcher, & Parker (2004)	MSCEIT (Mayer & Salovey 1997)	Pre/post-test	15 dentists and administrators attended a rope and challenge course	Mixed results
Sala (2006)	ECI (Goleman 1998)		19 participants from a large U.S. accounting firm and 20 Brazilian managers	Positive results
Groves, McEnrue, & Shen (2008)	EISDI (based on Mayer & Salovey 1997)		75 UG students on a 11-week leadership development program	1. Positive improvements in all four ability areas
Turner & Lloyd-Walker (2008)	ECI (Goleman 1998)	Pre/post-test (6 months)		
Clarke (2007a)	MSCEIT (Mayer & Salovey 1997)	Pre/post (14 weeks) comparison group	64 MBA students on a 14-week team project	1. Positive results for only Using Emotions Ability moderated by frequency of attendance

effects for self-evaluations were at the 0.10% level of significance and a number of the peer-rated competences, when looked at individually, actually decreased (three at the 0.05% level and one at the 0.10% level of significance) following training. Statistically, significant changes were found in job satisfaction and job performance, although only at the 10% level of significance.

One study evaluated EI development interventions using both trait and mixed model emotional intelligence measures. Slaski and Cartwright (2003) presented the results of a study to investigate the impact of EI training, and whether increased EI also had a positive effect on health and well-being. Based on a sample of 60 retail managers, they evaluated the impact of five training programs delivered 1 day per week for 4 weeks, with 12 managers attending each program. A pre/post-test research design with a comparison group was used where training participants completed two measures of emotional intelligence, the EQ-i (Bar-On, 1997) and the EIQ (Dulewicz & Higgs, 2003) as well as three measures of health and well-being, and pre-training, which was repeated 6 months later. Fifty-two and forty-nine complete data sets were obtained from trainees and managers in a control group, respectively. A positive impact for the training was reported with statistically significant improvements found in the EI measures used (the overall EQ-i score and a number of its subscales, and similarly in the overall EIQ score and all except two of its subscales). Positive changes were also found in measures of health and well-being.

The remaining four studies all evaluated EI development interventions based upon Mayer and Salovey's (1997) ability model of emotional intelligence. Two of these, however, used self- and peer-assessed measures of emotional abilities. Based on a sample of 82 undergraduate students participating in self-directed teams as part of a 12-week organizational behavior course, Moriarty and Buckley (2003) reported positive findings for the impact of the intervention on EI. Using a pre/post-test research design and a team-based measure of emotional intelligence (the WEIP-5, Jordan & Troth, 2004), significant positive changes were found in one of the two self-assessed EI measures of EI abilities. Findings from the peer-assessed measures of EI showed statistically significant improvements in both EI ability dimensions. By contrast, scores obtained from a sample of 80 students participating in a control group showed no change. Similarly, Groves, McEnrue, and Shen (2008) reported the results of an 11-week undergraduate management course that incorporated a specific focus on emotional intelligence, based on a sample of 75 students in the experimental group and 60 students in a comparison group. Again using a self-report measure of EI abilities developed specifically by the authors (the emotional intelligence self description inventory (EISDI)), statistically significant improvements in all four EI ability scores and overall EI score were obtained. No statistically significant changes were found in the control group.

Instead of using self- and peer-reporting measures, both Meyer, Fletcher, & Parker (2004) and Clarke (2007b) used an ability-based test to assess emotional intelligence (the Mayer-Salovey-Caruso-Emotional Intelligence Test (MSCEIT)), which is widely recognized as perhaps the most robust and valid measure of emotional intelligence currently available (Roberts, Zeidner & Matthews, 2001). Both studies reported mixed results with positive effects found only in a few of the emotional abilities examined. Meyer et al. (2004) evaluated the affects of a 1-day adventure (outward bound) training program on a sample of 15 dentists and administrators and found that positive effects on emotional abilities varied according to the subgroup of trainees. Clarke (2007b) undertook a larger study involving 64 MBA students participating in a 14-week self-directed team project and 13 students participating in a comparison group. Positive effects were only found for the ability of using emotions to facilitate thinking, but this was only for those students who had participated in team learning more intensively (that is, attended team meetings once per week or more). No statistically significant changes were found in the comparison group.

Based upon these studies, it would seem that developmental interventions can have an impact on emotional intelligence, but that the criterion measure used to assess emotional intelligence would appear to make a difference. Far more positive results are found for those studies using self- and peer-assessed measures of emotional intelligence irrespective of the EI model used (Groves, McEnrue, & Shen, 2008; Moriarty & Buckley, 2003; Sala, 2006; Slaski & Catrwright, 2003; Turner & Lloyd-Walker, 2008) but these suffer with validity problems due to the social desirability effects of self-reporting. Only two studies from those mentioned previously have used what might be considered more objective ability tests of emotional intelligence, and the findings here are far more cautious regarding the potential impact of development interventions (Clarke, 2007b; Meyer, Fletcher, & Parker, 2004). Despite suggestions in the literature, then, that training may have a positive effect on emotional intelligence (Bagshaw, 2000; Cherniss & Caplan, 2001; Clark, Callister, & Wallace, 2003; Dulewicz & Higgs, 2004; Watkin, 2000), there is in effect a paucity of data available to reach any confident conclusions. It is also difficult to determine from these studies in what ways the duration of any development intervention plays a role in their effectiveness. From those studies previously reported, positive effects were found as a result of both relatively short durations occurring fairly intensively over 1 to 2 days (Meyer, Fletcher, & Parker, 2004; Sala, 2006; Turner & Lloyd-Walker, 2008), as well as those occurring over a longer time frame such as over 5 (Slaski & Catrwright, 2003), 10 (Groves, McEnrue & Shen, 2008), 11 (Moriarty & Buckley, 2003) and even 14 weeks (Clarke, 2007b). Given the significant cost and resource implications associated with longer-term development interventions, identifying what effects, if any, targeted, short-term programs might have on emotional intelligence, is clearly of importance.

There is also a further theoretical issue to consider. Given that a significant amount of research to date is showing positive relationships between more objectively measured emotional intelligence *abilities* and behaviors associated with teamwork and leadership, major questions concerning the use of appropriate criterion measures for evaluating training effects must be addressed. It would seem to follow that in order to maintain theoretical and empirical consistency, far more studies are needed that focus on identifying whether and how emotional intelligence *abilities* develop and if so, under what conditions. It should not be expected that training results showing improvements in one type of EI measure will necessarily translate into the benefits expected as a result of research based upon completely different EI measures. Given that only two EI development studies have to date been conducted using objective ability test measures of EI, further studies using this measure are clearly needed.

From a project management perspective, there is also a need for studies that examine EI development interventions and whether these can be tracked to improvements in the attitudes and behaviors necessary for project management. Despite significant interest in the concept of emotional intelligence within project management (Drukat & Druskat, 2006), this is still a relatively unexplored concept within the field. Although some progress has been made in examining relationships between emotional intelligence and project management behaviors associated with leadership (Muller & Turner, 2007), research examining interventions for developing emotional intelligence in project managers is very much embryonic. The findings from the one evaluation study so far conducted by Turner and Lloyd-Walker (2008), although using a competence-based measure of emotional intelligence, also suggest that designing training interventions that are targeted specifically for project management may be an important factor to consider in maximizing the effectiveness of any training. They based their training on standard, generic training content rather than on specifically contextualized training for project management and found some positive effects in relation to some self-report measures. However, they also obtained negative effects or no changes with respect to peer report measures of EI.

For some time, it has been recognized in the training literature that learning is more likely to be supported more closely when the training content is able to mirror the actual work environment or job role (Baldwin & Ford, 1988). EI training that is far more contextualized and seeks to examine the use of emotional intelligence abilities within relevant and particular job contexts, may therefore be more effective. Turner and Lloyd-Walker (2008) also found no effects for the impact of EI training on job performance measures, although improvements were found on project managers' job satisfaction 6 months later. Far more research examining links between EI training and its effects on particular project management attitudes and behaviors is therefore needed.

4.3 Focus of the Current Study

The second component of the pilot study therefore aimed to evaluate the effectiveness of an emotional intelligence training program designed specifically for project managers. The focus of the study was to address the following objectives:

(1) To determine whether training can result in improvements in project managers' emotional intelligence abilities and relevant project management competences.

(2) To identify factors that may be associated with the effectiveness of emotional intelligence training.

Three specific hypotheses tested in the study and their rationale were as follows:

In relation to the development of emotional intelligence abilities, positive effects have been previously found for short-term training interventions targeting emotional accuracy recognition (Elfenbein, 2006) as well as with some branches of emotional intelligence abilities contained in the four-ability model (Meyer, Fletcher & Parker 2004). By contrast, findings from both quantitative and qualitative studies investigating the development of emotional abilities through workplace learning approaches have suggested that development is more likely to occur over a far longer time period involving a number of months or more (Clarke, 2006a, 2007b; Groves, McEnrue, & Shen, 2008; Moriarty & Buckley, 2003). Clarke (2007b) previously suggested that emotional intelligence training may provide trainees with an initial awareness of their emotional abilities, but that this is only a platform from which further development may occur as a result of learning which occurs on the job (workplace learning).This occurs as a result of trainees bringing their EI abilities to a more conscious awareness in their approaches to dealing with emotional experiences in the workplace, a process Clarke (2006a) refers to as "emotional knowledge work." Given that projects are increasingly recognized as emotional places (Chen, 2006; Peslak, 2005), participation in projects should subsequently offer significant opportunities for EI development. Based on this reasoning, training should not be expected to have any immediate effects on emotional intelligence abilities, but only after a period of some months has elapsed and participants have engaged in further workplace learning opportunities arising from participating in project work. This gives rise to the following hypothesis:

> *Hypothesis 6:* Positive changes in the emotional intelligence abilities (1) perceiving emotions, (2) using emotions to facilitate thinking, and (3) understanding emotions, will not be found immediately after participants have attended training but will be found 6 months later.

Although suggested as lying outside the ability construct of emotional intelligence, the dispositional tendency of empathy has been proposed as a characteristic of emotionally intelligent behavior (Salovey & Mayer, 1990). Previous studies have found moderate correlations between ability emotional intelligence and self-judgments of empathetic feeling (Brackett et al., 2006; Caruso, Mayer, & Salovey, 2002) suggesting it is a related but independent construct. Empathy involves a capacity for recognizing feelings in others, which requires a level of emotional awareness. Empathy, therefore, depends on the ability to perceive emotions (Mayer, Roberts, & Barsade, 2008). We should therefore expect to see increases in participant measures of empathy as a result of increases in their emotional intelligence abilities. This gives rise to the following hypothesis:

> *Hypothesis 7:* Significant increases in participants' empathetic ability will be detected 6 months following participants' training, but not immediately after training.

A number of authors have suggested that emotional intelligence may be an important aspect of individual difference that is associated with the skills and competences necessary for working in and leading projects (Druskat & Druskat, 2006; Muller & Turner, 2007; Leban & Zulauf, 2004). Turner and Lloyd-Walker (2008) have previously suggested that training in emotional intelligence should influence project managers' performance, and Mount (2006) found that emotional intelligence competences accounted for 69% of the variation in the skill set which project managers considered to be key for successful projects. The findings from study one presented earlier showed that emotional intelligence abilities were associated with the two project management competence areas of teamwork and conflict management. Significant changes in these two specific project management competences should therefore be expected as a result of improvements in participants' emotional intelligence abilities through training. This gives rise to the final hypothesis:

> *Hypothesis 8*: Training will result in positive improvements in project management behaviors (competences) associated with teamwork and conflict management 6 months following training, but not immediately after training.

4.3.1 The Training Intervention

This comprised a 2-day training program that was designed to improve a number of targeted emotional abilities and empathy among the participants specifically within a project management context. The training program was delivered on three separate occasions to three groups of project managers. Two groups of project managers were drawn from two organizations that were approached to participate in the study. The third group comprised participants from the UK chapter of the Project Management Institute who responded to an advertisement to take part in the research project. The total population of trainees combined both those attending voluntarily and those requested to attend by their organizations. It was expected that positive change in EI abilities should occur after 6 months and that this should also result in improvements in the three project management competence areas assessed. A comprehensive explanation of the theoretical underpinnings informing the development of the training, the nature of the content, and details of the material covered are provided in section six.

4.4 The Study and Methods

The study employed a pre/post-test quasi-experimental design (Campbell & Stanley, 1963) with measures of emotional intelligence collected 1 month prior to participants attending the 2-day EI training program (Time 1), again 1 month following the training (Time 2), and then again 6 months post training (Time 3). There were 57 project managers enrolled to take part in the training study. In addition, 18 project managers volunteered to act as a comparison group by completing measures but not attending training. Major problems with participant attrition resulted in only 36 complete data sets being obtained (containing measures from all three time points). A larger number (53) of the matched baseline and second postcourse (6 months later) were obtained, however. In order to maximize the statistical power of the tests, it was decided to run two sets of independent tests. The first set examined differences between all baseline measures and those obtained six months later using the larger data set ($n=53$). The second examined differences between the baseline and the first set of postcourse measures collected 1 month following training from the smaller subset ($n=36$). The characteristics of the larger sample of 53 training participants were as follows: the majority, 32 of these participants, were female (60%) and 15 (28%) were certified project managers; and the average age was 39.7 (SD 8.3) and ages ranged between 23 and 58. These participants indicated their job roles as follows: general management 14 (26%), marketing/sales 2 (4%), HRM/training 1 (2%), finance 2 (4%), R&D 2 (4%), technical 4 (8%), and other 28 (52%). Significant attrition was also encountered with the comparison group with matched baseline and 6 month postcourse measures obtained from only 6 of the 18 project managers volunteering to take part. As a result, it was decided to exclude data from the comparison group from subsequent analyses.

4.4.1 Dependent Measures

The following competences were assessed:

1) Emotional intelligence. The Mayer-Salovey-Caruso Emotional Intelligence Test (MSCEIT V2.0) (Mayer & Salovey, 1997) was used to assess the three emotional intelligence abilities: perceiving emotions, using emotions to facilitate thinking, and understanding emotions. Each of the three abilities is comprised of two task areas. The first exercise, the face-and-pictures tasks, required respondents to indicate the extent to which emotions were indicated by the visual stimuli, rated on a five-point Likert scale. Two tasks that assess the ability of using emotions to facilitate thinking ask respondents to consider the utility of certain emotions for facilitating behaviors (facilitation task) and judge comparisons between emotions being felt by an individual in a scenario to colors and temperature (sensations task). Two additional tasks, labeled as *changes* and *blends* tasks, require respondents to identify possible reactions given an individual's emotional state and to indicate how more basic emotions might combine to form more complex ones. Previously, reliabilities for each of the scales have been reported as 0.90, 0.76, and 0.77 (Mayer, Salovey, & Caruso, 2002). Reliabilities obtained for each of the three branches on the first administration were 0.88, 0.62, and 0.95, respectively. At the second administration, coefficient scores were 0.89, 0.57, and 0.90, respectively.

2) Empathy. Mehrabian and Epstein's (1972) 33-item of emotional empathy was used to assess empathetic tendency. Responses to each item are on a scale ranging from +4 (very strong agreement) to −4 (very strong disagreement). Scores on 17 items are negatively scored, in that the signs of a participant's response on negative items are changed. A total empathy score is then obtained by adding all 33 items. Sample items include: (1) (+) "It makes me sad to see a lonely stranger in a group"; and (24) (−) "I am able to make decisions without being influenced by people's feelings." The scale authors previously reported the split-half reliability for the measure as 0.84. Here the Spearman-Brown split-half coefficient was found to be 0.86, suggesting good reliability.

3) Project Management Competences. The teamwork competence was assessed using a 7-item scale. Sample items included: (1) Built trust and confidence with both stakeholders and others involved on the project?; and (2) Helped to create an environment of openness and consideration on the project? Conflict management was assessed using a six-item scale. Sample items included: (1) Recognized conflict; and (2) Worked effectively with the organizational politics associated with the project. Reliability coefficients were found to be satisfactory at 0.82 and 0.79 for each of the two scales, respectively.

4.4.1.1 *Qualitative Data*

The collection of qualitative alongside quantitative data, in evaluating training interventions, is recommended as a means to gain more in-depth insights into both the impact of training and factors associated with its effectiveness (Clarke, 2002). It also offers a means to triangulate findings from a range of differing sources, thereby strengthening the validity of findings (Denzin & Lincoln, 1994). Semi-structured interviews were therefore undertaken with a subset of the 53 individuals from which baseline and final sets of measures were collected from the 3 training programs. In order to randomize the selection process, an individual with no prior knowledge of the project was asked to select 20 names from three lists of training participants representing those that attended each of the three training courses. Fifteen of these individuals were willing and able to take part in the follow-up interviews 6 months following the training. Interviews lasted between 25 and 45 minutes and were held at the place of work of the participant. Each interview was recorded and shorthand notes were taken by the researcher. A semi-structured interview schedule (Appendix 1) was devised which made use of the critical incident technique approach (Flanagan, 1954). This minimizes risks of generic or socially desirable responses and focuses on identifying specific behavioral data. The interviews were structured so as to capture how specific behaviors, thinking processes, or attitudes which are associated with EI had changed as a result of the training. At the end of each interview, the researcher summarized key points covered in the interviews based on the shorthand notes and checked for a common understanding with the respondent in order to verify the data obtained.

4.4.1.2 *Data Analyses*

1) Quantitative Data. Initial tests began with examining correlations between all variables measured in the study collected at the baseline and 6 months later. This was followed by undertaking a multivariate analysis of variance using a repeated measures design (MANOVA). Time was entered as the subject factor name with two levels (pre- and 6-month post test) alongside the six dependent variables assessed in the study: three EI abilities, empathy, and the two project manager competences). Initial positive results suggested follow-up univariate analyses were necessary. The software programme SPSS for Windows (Version 15.0; SPSS Chicago, IL, USA) was used for all statistical analyses.

2) Qualitative Data. All interview tapes were initially transcribed and then analyzed using a semi-emergent theme approach (Denzin & Lincoln, 1994, Miles & Huberman, 1994). In the first phase, all transcripts were initially read through by the researcher and the process of coding was begun by initially identifying and categorizing data that captured training impact and effectiveness (Coffey & Atkinson, 1996; Creswell, 1998). In the second phase, transcripts were analyzed further to identify any key themes that were common across interviews and which were not covered in the coding frame. In the third phase, these emergent themes were then coded into broader constructs where linkages were present. In order to maximize the trustworthiness of the inferences drawn from the qualitative data by the researcher, coding matrices containing the data were then presented to two additional researchers who were not involved in the project. Data were then retained when there was common agreement on the inferences drawn, and where the analysis from across the interviews converged. Excerpts from interview transcripts were selected based on judgments from all three researchers regarding those that offered richer details to best illustrate the findings.

4.5 Results

Means, standard deviations, and correlations between measures are presented in Table 9. The number of significant correlations between each of the three emotional abilities B1, B2, and B3, confirm that these abilities are related to one another within an overall construct, emotional intelligence. Initial MANOVA tests were performed to identify whether any statistically significant changes had occurred in measures of the dependent variables between pre- and 6-month post-training. Results indicated significant differences had occurred between the two time points, $(F [6,47] = 4.45, p < 0.001)$. Further follow-up univariate analyses of variance tests were therefore conducted (Table 10). The results for the emotional abilities of perceiving emotions $(F [6,47] = 0.08, < n.s.])$ and using emotions to facilitate thinking $(F [6,47] = 0.55, p < n.s.)$, failed to show any statistically significant changes. Significant effects were found, however, in relation to the emotional ability, understanding emotions $(F (6,47) = 7.76, p < 0.01)$. Follow-up t-tests on differences between baseline and first post-test measures (1 month following training) showed no statistically significant changes in any of the three emotional abilities. Perceiving emotions, $t(35) = -0.1, p < n.s.$; using emotions $t(35) = 0.21, p < n.s.$, and understanding emotions, $t(35) = -0.38, p < n.s.$ Hypothesis 6 was therefore partially supported.

Significant differences were also found between the baseline and the 6-month post-training measures of empathy $(F [6,45] = 3.96, p < 0.05)$. Follow-up t-tests on differences between baseline and first post-test measures (1 month following training) showed no statistically significant changes, empathy $t(35) = 1.84, p < n.s.$ However, an examination of the mean scores obtained for baseline and 6-month post-test measures (Table 11) shows that empathy scores actually decreased over this time period. Hypothesis 7 was therefore not supported. Finally, significant positive changes were also found between the baseline and 6-month post-course measures in both of the project management competences of teamwork $(F [6,45] =$

Table 9. Correlations Between All Variables (Time 1 and Time 2)

	1	2	3	4	5	6	7	8	9	10	11
1. (B1) Perceive											
2. (B2) Use	0.57**										
3. (B3) Understand	0.26	0.49**									
4. Empathy	0.11	0.27	0.27								
5. Teamwork	0.24	0.46**	0.39**	0.23							
6. Conflict management	0.14	0.38**	0.36**	0.04	0.76**						
7. B1 (2)	0.68**	0.63**	0.43**	0.06	0.29*	0.18					
8. B2 (2)	0.49**	0.67**	0.42**	0.22	0.38**	0.35*	0.39**				
9. B3 (3)	0.02	0.20	0.47**	-0.05	0.47**	0.41**	0.17	0.015			
10. Empathy (2)	0.06	0.27*	0.23	0.78**	0.21	0.09	0.14	0.27	0.06		
11. Teamwork (2)	0.23	0.36**	0.29**	0.27	0.48**	0.31*	0.22	0.24	0.11	0.22	
12. Conflict management (2)	0.15	0.22	0.21	0.44**	0.45**	0.26	0.06	0.23	0.13	0.36**	0.68**

$*p < 0.05$, $**p < 0.01$

Table 10. Results of Univariate *F* Tests on Emotional Abilities, Empathy, and Project Management Competences

Variable	Type III Sum of Squares	DF	F	Significance	Partial η^2
Perceiving emotions (B1)	10.41	1	0.08	0.78	0.002
Using emotions (B2)	40.68	1	0.55	0.46	0.01
Understand emotions (B3)	324.67	1	7.66	0.008	1.28
Empathy	456.60	1	3.96	0.05	0.07
Teamwork	0.813	1	4.34	0.04	0.08
Managing conflict	1.98	1	6.27	0.01	0.11

4.34, $p < 0.05$), and conflict management (F [6,45] = 6.27, $p < 0.01$). Follow up *t*-tests on differences between baseline and first post-test measures (1 month following training) showed no statistically significant changes in any of these competences, teamwork $t(35) = 1.31$, $p <$ n.s.; or managing conflict, $t(35) = .06$, $p <$ n.s. Hypothesis 8 was therefore supported.

4.5.1 Findings From the Qualitative Data

The presentation of the qualitative data is organized within four broad categories that offer insights into both the impact of the EI training and factors associated with its effectiveness. These are as follows: (1) impact of the training on participants' emotional intelligence ability of understanding emotions; (2) impact of the training on participants' motivation to use emotional intelligence; (3) impact of the EI training on project manager competences of managing conflict and teamwork; and (4) factors associated with the effectiveness of the EI training.

Table 11. Means and Standard Deviations of Dependent Variables Pre- and 6-Months Posttraining

Variable	Pretraining	1 month post-training*	6 months post-training**
Perceiving emotions (B1)	93.77 (18.64)	95.77 (22.05)	94.39 (20.80)
Using emotions (B2)	95.78 (14.64)	97.70 (14.52)	94.54 (15.41)
Understand emotions (B3)	97.85 (9.37)	99.24 (9.30)	101.35 (8.5)
Empathy	30.16 (22.97)	28.52 (21.53)	26.0 (23.33)
Teamwork	5.63 (0.64)	5.64 (0.72)	5.81 (0.55)
Managing conflict	5.53 (0.69)	5.43 (0.43)	5.59 (0.70)

*$N = 36$, **$N = 53$.

4.5.1.1. *Impact of the EI Training on Participant's Emotional Intelligence Ability of Understanding Emotions*

There were many examples evident from the interviews with project managers that offer strong support for the key finding from the quantitative data analysis, that there had been improvements in the emotional ability of understanding emotions. A key impact of the training appeared to have been in encouraging participants to consider, in advance, the emotional impact of specific work-related scenarios and situations, and where possible, to attempt to plan ahead about how these might be best managed. Although not in themselves evidence of development of this ability, the qualitative data suggests a far more active use of this ability by training participants than had been the case prior to their attending the training program:

"There was one thing that came out of the training, about emotion being contagious. I think I recognize that now... I used to actually get quite worked up about something and think 'Why is she not speaking to me? Have I done something wrong?' and take it all quite personally. But now I tend to actually allow for it a lot more, I can understand why...and probably try and approach it in a different way. If I need something, whereas before I would've said 'I'm not even going to talk to her because you know I must have upset her,' now I understand what it is and say, 'Well, I do need something from her and someone is gonna have to talk to her but in a different way.' So I say, 'I know you are really busy and trying to meet a deadline but I really need this in order to be able to continue with my work if you like,' whereas before I would have tended to let it slip 2 or 3 days before I got the information from her, which would hold my work up." (Project Manager male A1)

"Something that's been going on a lower level way for possibly a couple of years but it recently rose its head about 3 months ago...so I wanted to understand what I had to do in a situation like that...I thought about how I wanted to handle the situation, which I kind of planned out and put to my line manager...however, I had anticipated and the training reoccurred to me at each step of the way. Thinking about how the individual was likely to respond to the things that we were putting in place—which is not normally how I act—I normally just...deal with it and then what comes back can sometimes be quite a surprise. Whereas this time I was thinking, 'I think it's likely that he won't want to do this—that he will want to propose something else.' I thought, 'He is likely to respond like this.' I had a very uneasy feeling about meeting him, I didn't want to meet him and I asked my line manager if he would meet him instead of me. Not in despair of avoidance, but I had a kind of instinct surrounding it." (Project Manager female A7)

"I really had to understand what might be making this line manager act the way she is towards her staff and I know that there's been incidents in the past...and it's not obvious, the person doesn't come across that way, and you just wouldn't expect it really...I do find it hard to understand why she would do that...so I don't know I have tried to understand what might motivate someone to act in such way to upset people so much...I haven't actually succeeded in changing the situation but I think I know much more about [the dynamics] that's causing all this." (Project Manager female A19)

One of the salient findings to arise from the qualitative data was the extent to which understanding emotions was being actively used by these project managers, particularly as part of their role in relationship management:

"...We had a project that we've been working on—its in its fourth year. An international project with a number of partners and collaborators. And it's had kind of what you would say is a rough history of relationships. It's not an instinctive relationship...it's more a kind of structured relationship where we decided 'wouldn't this model be good to try?'...But there's been a lot of disagreements along the way: how it should be resourced and how it should be structured, and one partner pulled out of it because they didn't like the way it was going. And it broke down. But some of the learning from the training I applied to it. It was quite soon after we had had the training and I was thinking about the need for clear boundaries and thinking about how emotions were driving things. We hadn't set it up contractually right. We hadn't written things down or been very clear with the partners about exactly what we expected of them and what they expected of us. There was so much breakdown in communication and lots of e-mails flying around about which, you know, you miss a lot about what we talked about on the training, tone, and meaning...And you can't see how people are responding or reacting. And everybody said, 'There's no time to meet and we should pull the project,' and I said, 'No. We need to make every attempt.' I suggested a face to face meeting and no one wanted to do it but I insisted that a face to face was really important because of the crisis....it didn't fundamentally resolve all the issues, but we put practical things in place and worked together to plan how would we tackle the quality of relationships. It was quite rewarding to see people coming together and wanting it to succeed basically and moving from their position of pulling it...It was fantastic—absolutely fabulous, very successful." (Project Manager female A3)

"...Some of the work that I've done since then has actually been working with third parties and partners, with some of them being quite challenging. So it's been useful to try to convey messages in a positive way so we end up with the best end result...trying to understand how my actions and body language can either help or detract from what we're trying to achieve." (Project Manager male A12)

"...Setting up this program—I mean it's a huge program—it's a lot of money and we have ten pilots all over the country now. Very quickly literally within 2 months, we had to write a business plan for the next 3 years. And certainly it really meant that we had to establish trust very early on, and I thought, 'Well, probably the best thing to do is visit them...[I said] 'I just want to sit down with you for 2½ hours, 3 hours, whatever time you've got, and you just tell me everything you can'; and that created a kind of quality to the relationship...I think that, yeah, the relationships are based on trust and that trust was about sitting down and kind of going to their location." (Project Manager female A19)

"One quite interesting project where...I was working for lots of different people...and I guess I played different hands with each person...and how just being really aware of where I was with each person and working on each relationship made a massive difference. I guess I'm much more aware of the emotional situation and this has had a massive effect on how I'd be dealing with people. Certainly when they do me a favor as well, and its beyond their job description, certainly...really just understanding how the other person may feel... 'not another e-mail from him,' which I know a lot of the time people would be thinking...so I'm very very mindful now of how my requests may influence things...and work so that the relationship stays good and they are still willing to help me out. (Project Manager male A5)

"I'm generally known as being fairly open-minded, and what we're trying, working with a particular client, is to demonstrate that in terms of being open-minded. To listen to their problems, thinking through all kinds of issues, the priorities that they have. Before we then try to find a mutual solution. It's a difficult balance because sometimes we have the representation without responsibility, or the power to actually agree on something. So quite often it's just trying to listen. Trying to keep the balance without giving away anything. But actually bringing that back to the main organization as a potential difficulty with some potential solutions and trying to agree so that negotiations on this side can work. It's actually been something that has been quite difficult in the last 6 months but I do feel that the training has helped me to improve on that." (Project Manager male B6)

4.5.1.2 *Impact of the Training on Participants' Motivation to Use Emotional Intelligence*

A major finding to emerge from the qualitative data was that attendance of the training appeared to have some impact on these project managers' motivation to use emotional intelligence abilities. This seemed to occur in a number of ways. Gaining an increased awareness of emotional intelligence and how it may influence leadership and management within projects may have provided a means for directing cognitive attention to use knowledge and skills in this area. This included a heightened awareness of the need to address the emotional impact of work situations and a consideration of strategies for doing so. For some, this also involved a far more personal shift in how they dealt with emotional situations arising in the course of work:

> "But what you left with, is the kind of emotional situations that everybody kind of has in their own particular way, and struggles in this area in their everyday work. And then if you don't tackle them, they don't really go away; so I think I learnt a lot about how you need to manage the emotional part of situations. To look at ways of talking things through with colleagues. So I think that's what stuck really." (Project Manager female B4)

> "Ah, the main fact I really brought from it was that emotions are the one thing which really aren't discussed at work and how they almost go completely ignored. Although learning from it they are perhaps, fundamentally, the most important things that humans endure, and can kind of make or break an organization...certainly they can either add to or detract from a successful team or department." (Project Manager male A8)

> "I think it's become much more visible and palpable to me now in all kinds of situations I used to think which is probably what attracted me to the training in the first place; that I had kind of always felt that I was quite good at gauging the temperature in terms of morale, moods in the workplace. I would have thought that I picked up on those very quickly and quite early...But now I kind of feel after that training that there is a lot going on under the surface for a lot of people. And how some people have difficulty with expressing that. But now what I do see very much is our reluctance at times to act, which is very interesting, but not always good." (Project Manager female B13)

> "Ah, I definitely am a lot more conscious about emotions and being able to be quite upfront about that and saying, 'Look we work in an incredibly emotional [arena]...' and, I kind of see it all a bit more clearly now, and I guess there's a larger awareness in general that does affect me on a day to day..." (Project Manager female C7)

A number of training participants were able to identify specific situations that occurred since attending the training where this increased awareness of emotional intelligence caused them to do things differently:

"There have been staff situations, in large meetings where you realize that the dynamics aren't going that great—it's a bit anxious, and you think about what your role is in intervening and whether you should or shouldn't, and how you should tackle it. What the best way? So although what the training has taught me is that you kind of need to prepare and you actually need to be able to think about these things in order to be prepared." (Project Manager female A7).

"[A colleague was] giving a presentation on a very key piece of work to a critical deadline...and I felt that people's anxiety levels had been building...and it was very badly done...in terms of communicating the message...And it started to deteriorate—he didn't pick up on how badly it was going down...I realized the situation was deteriorating but there's 30 people in the room, including managers...the staff were being very negative and unconstructive about it...and asking questions that weren't helpful...And I remember picking up on the discomfort, feeling uncomfortable...and thinking I need to try and alleviate the situation; to intervene in some way." (Project Manager female B11)

There was also some evidence that the structured skill sessions on the training program played a role in increasing these project managers' self-efficacy in being able to deal with emotional situations. For some, this was communicated by suggesting they now felt more confident in dealing with emotional situations which previously they might have avoided:

"Ah, I think just the way I deal with big groups, I was always, well it was a new group and I'm quite shy. I tend to just kind of go in and sit, and wait to hear everybody else...and I was the center of attention in one of the meetings...I actually had to give a speech and it was quite good although I was still a little nervous...so now in meetings I actually try to suggest ideas and get conversations flowing...And when there are meetings with people more senior, I have been trying to put myself to the front a bit more." (Project Manager male B2)

"On a very personal level, it is more acknowledging that if I was feeling in a particular way, to actually go with it, rather than just say ok and just ignore how I'm feeling...and if the emotions persist, to act upon them, which is something that I've never done before. And I've taken a very different slant, which means that I'm willing to get myself into some confrontational situations or in situations where I perhaps have never been quite so bold or brave. So I guess it's really helped, in a way it's developed new thoughts...giving me a lot more confidence in myself and what I'm doing and thinking...also in terms of having a conflict with a member of my team I actually stood up to and really really taking it forward and not backing away from it despite its being incredibly uncomfortable and difficult. Taking that step I feel better if I actually move on what I'm feeling rather than sort of stand back and cower behind my emotions." (Project Manager male A5)

Although the data did not suggest any improvement in terms of development of the two emotional abilities, perceiving emotions and using emotions to facilitate thinking, the qualitative data did suggest that these abilities were being used by project managers. The motivational aspects of the training program may have impacted the performance of some emotional abilities even though there was no evidence for their development. For example, in relation to perceiving emotions, there was some indication that training participants were more aware of body language and how this might offer insights into how others might be feeling.

"How people react to what other people are saying, not just their voices but also the way they were physically reacting as well...and sometimes when they are under pressure, when they are trying to negotiate something, when they weren't getting what they wanted...I mostly have to deal with handling people who are not interested in what you are saying, and trying to just work ways around that, and kind of trying to negotiate their feelings..." (Project Manager male B2)

"Body language, I have become very much more aware of that now and I have spotted it in lots of places, and if I see people copying stuff I'm just more aware. I don't think it changes how I read the situation but I'm definitely more aware of it." (Project Manager female B11).

"This member of the team who came to me, I mean I could kind of read the situation from how he was, and I actually went to him and I said, 'Are you ok? Because I'm not really sure that you are.' And I guess I felt prepared to be able to deal with that situation if you know what I mean, I didn't want to upset him, I just said, 'you know, let's try and work this through...' I think it did allow us to chart a plan...so I guess it allowed us to plot a way through that situation." (Project Manager female A19)

Also in terms of perceiving their own emotional states:

"I guess it gave me a measure of the other person, to say, 'Look, I'm feeling terrible my motivation has disappeared...' I was honest, at least I won't go back to where there would be a situation now or in the future where I wish I'd said this or that, wish I had explained how I felt, or expressed myself fully...in a way if you don't speak your thoughts then they just stay inside and then tend to be more self damaging rather than if you are aware of them so that you can move on." (Project Manager male A16).

There was some indication that a number of trainees were far more aware of their emotions and appeared to be more consciously making use of this knowledge in relation to decision making:

> "I think definitely just acknowledging that my emotions at work actually exist, that's something I had always tried to almost remove except for the positive ones. But I think it's me acknowledging the negative ones too that's really the main difference. I do have rubbish days and some days where...I think they're the days not to make decisions or to avoid certain types of tasks...so sometimes having a stronger knowledge of how I feel and knowing how to apply myself more effectively to certain tasks that I've got I can just get a remarkable amount of things done..." (Project Manager male A5)

> "The meeting went very badly and, probably very uncharacteristic of me, I was virtually silent the whole way through which is not my style at all. So when we came out of the meeting...and it was very distressing...I felt it was kind of left opened ended and a bit unsatisfactory so I tackled the manager about that, tackle isn't the right word probably, and we disagreed fundamentally about the way it had gone and the way that we wanted it to go forward...and it was playing on my mind and actually I don't feel good that it hasn't been resolved, so it's kind of left in the air, I'm not really happy about it...so I'm left with the decision about whether to act, which is really about dealing with how I'm feeling..." (Project Manager female A7)

The processing of emotional information here also seems an important catalyst underpinning problem solving. This includes a focus on how individuals might change their own behaviors in order to deal with particular relationships in the future. Emotions, combined with the abilities of emotional awareness were therefore intimately associated with the process of critical reflection for many of these trainees. Specific examples were identified of emotionally driven problem solving as part of critical reflection that led to theorizing about how to improve interpersonal relationships:

> "...It's not a complimentary one to me but I've unpicked my behavior subsequently. I had a meeting with someone from outside the organization and we were going to talk about strategy. We were all working on a common project with different elements of that strategy and I thought I was meeting this person to talk about our alignment so we were all getting the same messages even though we were coming from different departments if you like. This person proceeded to interrogate me and interviewed me about the work that I was doing. I could see my body language was becoming like this, I was moving my eye contact away, I was turning away...I was very defensive...so I'm

thinking, 'Why we've got all this interrogation coming my way? To fill the space in terms of what you haven't done? But I have to admit that I did not handle that situation well. I recognize my behaviors were defensive...when I am responding in a defensive way that's impeding my cognitive ability to deal with the situation and my feelings at the same time...Subsequently I thought of the strategies—you know: I didn't have an agenda for the meeting, I didn't know this person, the agreement was not there that we'll be talking about, they came on in a hierarchical way to try to impose something even though we were equals so, I was unassertive and I'm really surprised because I'm really an assertive person and I became unassertive. But I analyzed it and I know I'll have some strategies the next time." (Project Manager female C9)

"I'm actually conscious sometimes of not trying to make the effort, and that...it actually takes a tremendous amount to match reasoning with the emotional stuff. It was easier to say let's forget it, let's call it a day. However realizing why I felt the way I did a lot more, I went ahead and took that decision. And I've been proved wrong because (the person) after one meeting was wonderful." (Project Manager female A7)

Examples were also found where trainees had drawn upon their emotional states to reflect upon their own behaviors, and how these may have either positive or negative emotional impacts within their projects or teams. Importantly there was a clear focus found here with trainees considering action strategies that were associated with more effective emotional regulation:

"It's difficult to try and remain on a professional play level field. I won't go into any details but I have had some quite difficult situations personally, and this affected my behavior and my mood at times. So I do find myself sometimes consciously trying to switch from being me, to walking into a room as the calmed professional. Oh, I think once or twice yes, I've been a bit 'short' with people, but I'm generally more balanced when I'm actually with a client. With the team I work with, sometimes all that spills over, and that's inevitable. I can't pretend to switch off all the time. But I do feel with the people that I work with I've got enough trust and they've got enough trust in me to discuss things if needed...Yeah once or twice the language can get a bit colorful which is a way of my letting off steam." (Project Manager male A12)

"There was conflict with a partner, [they] were seeking to change an agreement that we had made, and which had a potential impact of £ 700,000 of business for this company...and again trying to negotiate through that conflict, trying to remain calm, trying to remain definitive about what we're trying to achieve...I wouldn't normally lose my temper but I have actually been known to become quite assertive at times in this kind of situation...and I think maybe by remaining calm, with that level balance, that did actually help a lot." (Project Manager male A8)

"I suppose it's one way of looking at it, because instead of looking at a situation and stressing, you can actually understand what's causing that situation and say to yourself, 'I'm not gonna let myself get stressed by it.'" (Project Manager male A1)

"Yes, I have had a very difficult situation where a colleague has behaved very defensively but has tipped into aggression, as it often does when people are defensive...the person I felt has been incongruent...so I was losing trust very rapidly with that particular person...my instinct when I saw the person was to run away. It was a very powerful physical instinct as the person approached me...My feeling was to move away, physically move away or reduce eye contact. I was conscious of my behaviors and I worked very hard to mitigate against them..." (Project Manager female C9)

4.5.1.3 The Impact of the EI Training on Project Manager Competence of Teamwork and Managing Conflict

Emerging from the grounded analysis of the qualitative data was evidence that training participants had been using various aspects of emotional intelligence within the areas of communication and teamwork. Some were evidently far more aware that the way in which they communicate can have an emotional impact on those they work with in projects, and that this could potentially have both positive or negative impacts:

"Actually talking and dealing with some of the hard issues. That we are actually giving hard messages to people and some of the people that I work with. It's become easier with that kind of understanding and practice about how to convey some of the difficult messages about performance, and I think some of the actions suggested, about how to convey those messages in such a way that they will have positive emotional impacts rather than negative. I think that was actually very useful." (Project Manager male A8)

"...I think if I've learnt anything from the training is this notion of how you contribute in a good or a bad way to the kind of the situation that's goes down. So you can actively intervene to try and move it, shift the mood or the emotions. I mean emotions are strong, I'm not an avoider. I can deal with conflict and I'm not afraid if someone's emotional. But I think now its not as invisible as it was, and so I know for a fact that round the room everybody has got something going on and how something might be received very differently. So sometimes you have to manage that, and think about the perceptions and how it will affect people...and change the mood if you can." (Project Manager female C9)

"Yes, well, I think a lot more. I've been doing that since the training because I suppose that if you internalize a lot of what you imagine emotional intelligence to be...and I think what I've learnt is that actually you can take it much further than that. You can actively use it to improve situations. I think on a low level there are probably interactions all the time where you can try to understand where someone is coming from. We're not the best communicators entirely, we're kind of head down and very busy. So people would come up to you very abruptly and say, 'Have you got this, have you got that,' there are no niceties around that. So I suppose I have tried to kind of work with that." (Project Manager female A7)

"It's really that communication stuff, I think that's what I generally try to focus on, because I came from a technical background. I try to actually set that aside when I'm talking with people and not lose them about IT. And [the people focus], that's really helped me back out of some potential difficulties. To actually try and think, what's my audience? Who am I talking to and what kind of level?" (Project Manager male A16)

This increased awareness of the role emotions play in project management was also found in relation to how some project managers thought about improving teamwork:

"...I see (EI) as an extra tool to help me get by...even in the sense of, you know, making a team happier...I'm currently working in this project where I've been basically [put] into another team...I think we can just organize this whole team much better because everyone is flat. No-one is communicating. It looks really miserable. I'm trying to create a team, people working together, and they say, oh that's a great idea. So now that's fundamentally changed the whole engine dynamic...I guess I'm just more aware of how emotions really, really play a part in the success. People would be doing the same work, the same stuff but because their emotions are different, they would be doing their work differently...because if you are unhappy your mind is not where you are...it's somewhere else, so you make more mistakes...I certainly do... Just acknowledging I feel [lousy] and that's ok so it's not even about it's all happy. It's great, it's more about honesty, that sometimes things are bad you know its worth talking about." (Project Manager male A5)

"My background is in engineering, and I did a lot of early work in logic...I like logical systems, I try to defeat people logically all the time and it never works. I tried to set up systems. I'm quite good at enforcing them, which is basically my job, preventing things from getting too chaotic. But I think if you are very much aware of the emotional currency in a team, especially in a large organization or several organizations together, it actually helps you separate out from the systems. I think that's given me a greater clarity...and just being able to say, OK guys, this particular issue is about how we get from A to B, progress reports, or whatever. Let's get focused on the task and then we can also work on whatever issues that come of that in terms of how you're feeling, and I think that's how it helped, It has given me great clarity." (Project Manager female C9)

This also included project managers attempting to be more aware of how their team members may be feeling, suggesting some use of empathy:

"This is a vulnerable person that's just started in the team. I've got a long-established team. We get on really well. We've grown to be personal friends, and there are high levels of trust and I tried to put myself in the position of somebody trying very hard to break into that and be accepted into the group. You know, be part of that team, and this person has a high level of skills. The skills aren't in question. It is [the] other [person's] ways of operating, coming from a different organizational culture...So I tried very hard to put myself in that person's shoes, and this is not like another [sector's] processes. We've got business processes. We have to sell our time. We've got to count every minute of every day. And so I had to really work hard to feel what that must be like and to put the effort in to building the relationship." (Project Manager female C7)

"Yeah, I identified someone in the project. This is someone who has moved from central government to local government...This person now reports to me and that's an incredible change, and this guy, he just hasn't got there yet...But there are all kinds of problems because he still thinks he is central government and of course the power shift...but I remember in the transition I thought he is just going to be traumatized because he's going from a very high position really to this absolutely hell leather crazy delivery boat...and I think he was actually very vulnerable...because he feels destabilized in some way... I was trying to arrange visits...He phoned me out of panic and he said, 'There's no reason for you to come here...' But I know that he's still really irritated at a deep level, and I have to guard against that and be more [aware of it]." (Project Manager female A19)

"Yes I probably do that quite a bit now actually...Yes, especially when I'm thinking performance management and, well, when I'm giving feedback...I actually do consciously think how would the person be perceiving that news and, to make sure that I appreciate how they're feeling. I think to some extent I've done that for a long time but I'm just more consciously aware of it." (Project Manager female B11)

"...Well, I've been working closely with someone on a project, and, we had an issue. Both of us had an issue with one of the other people, much more senior on the project. And we got to the point where I think the issue is when you start to lose respect for somebody. You start to not empathize with them anymore. So my colleague was in quite a bad place about this whole situation. So I tried to work with her to find that core of respect for this person. We needed to empathize with where she's coming from and I think that's how we resolved it. We tried to empathize, sort of contextualize why she was behaving in that way..." (Project Manager female C9)

"...In terms of performance managing somebody that I actually worked with...I try to put myself into that situation and, yes, I try to guess how they might actually be feeling—how I can communicate and get across those issues..." (Project Manager male A12)

Given that the training program was designed around a specific focus on conflict within projects from which to analyze the use of emotional intelligence abilities, it was not surprising that many project managers identified how their skills and practice in this area had changed. Importantly these changes could be linked to the use of particular emotional intelligence abilities.

The first of these was understanding the emotional impact of situations within projects and how these might lead to relationship conflict. Recognizing this meant a number were far more active in planning how to manage potential conflict situations in order to manage the emotional outcomes:

"It's very structured about approaching situations like this and that was helpful to me because you've got to find your own way through it...You've got to find your own style, but the best thing was it actually encouraged us to plan and we did plan a very difficult conversation with this new member of staff...And it's fair because it offered the other person the chance to come back to us, but we've got the information beforehand, plan very carefully, and we shared out the roles. We were clear with ourselves who was chairing the meeting, and the air was cleared as a result...It was a very positive thing for everyone." (Project Manager female C7)

Others were able to recognize how a failure to effectively plan had meant they were far less effective at managing the emotional aspects that then led to conflict:

"Ah, yes there was one actually, when we were doing a project and putting a conference together, and there was quite a bit of conflict in the team as to who should be doing what. And where the roles really weren't defined early on in the project that caused considerable conflict in the team...but I think as I've reflected on it, I was able to think, well, actually it's because we weren't being an effective team because we hadn't agreed some issues on that project. We need to approach it in a different way at an earlier enough stage." (Project Manager female B11)

There was some evidence that a number of training participants were far more aware of the need to manage their own emotions in order to avoid conflict within their project teams:

"In my new team situation, I have somebody new who doesn't stick to the rules, who bends and twists, and I was quite angry with this person, who's had a lot of time off since she started...and I don't think I've got the full story as I was told some lies along the way...then when I discovered that I was being manipulated, I had my feelings that mixed up, genuine concern contrasting with this sort of anger, unimpressed that I had been let down...and then we had to go into this meeting... and I had to make an effort to manage my feelings so as to get to the end result." (Project Manager female C7).

"I did have a conflict situation and, unfortunately, it was me putting forward an argument that wasn't particularly listened to...and in this conflict situation I did try various tactics, being extremely balanced and direct, trying to be positive. But ultimately I felt...being resolution focused rather than just kicking out some grievances and hoping for the best helped." (Project Manager male A5)

4.5.1.4 *Factors associated with the effectiveness of the EI training*

When talking about their experience gained from attending the EI training, there were a number of instances where project managers referred to aspects of the design of the training that appeared to have had an influence on their learning. The first key aspect here was how the training had offered opportunities for participants to learn vicariously from others participating on the program:

"I found those situations very helpful, where you can observe and see how someone else does, and you can think, oh yes, that's a very good thing to try. So, in similar conflict situations, where you've got some difficult conversations to have with people, and I do that quite frequently in my job, I found the practice in a safe environment a very useful thing and looking to see how others deal with it...And it has been quite difficult for me because recently we had some very difficult conversations with [this person] so the training and the experience helped in building up my confidence levels to deal with that situation." (Project Manager female C7)

"What was most interesting was watching my colleagues actually interacting together, I think I learnt more about them watching them doing the exercises.. I didn't have that kind of insight of them before, so in a way that was one of my favorite things...but all kinds of things, you know, about body language and stuff. I mean, I took a lot away, you know, about understanding behavior...I guess I wouldn't have planned how I'd be using different bits of information but I learned to look at a deeper level, more conscious of observing people's interactions together." (Project Manager female A19)

The training also offered opportunities for sharing ideas from across the project management field more broadly:

"I did actually meet a couple of guys on the course that actually had some very similar issues and I think that cross fertilization could be built on because trying to work in a project management field, it's especially easy to get into a silo of where you are and what you're thinking. Some of the ideas the other guys were coming up with were very useful." (Project Manager male B6)

A number of participants also identified how the structured, facilitated sessions contained in the training enabled them to gain insights on their own behaviors and how their emotions were connected to them:

"Well another thing sticks in my mind. You remember the exercise when we sat in a circle with blindfolds on and there was a rope in the middle. And then you videoed this and played it back to us. I was horrified to see that I was leaping in there and I thought I had got this under control over the years, stopped doing that (laugh), because I'm always (laugh), I mean I think that it's a good thing about me, being very spontaneous, but it can be a double-edged sword. And I wish I was a bit more reflective and made more measured decisions. It's made me more conscious of that." (Project Manager female C7)

"I particularly enjoyed the role play sessions that we undertook, where we had to play games and adopt particular roles and the opportunities to feed back. What was very interesting to me was the videoing, that was very, very powerful to look at how people interact...Because I was blindfolded I didn't realize how many people just sat out that activity. In my video I saw I was quite in there—someone that's always in, and we just do it without thinking...And I thought, my goodness, there are a number of people in that scenario that either were disengaged from it, or for whatever reason—being uncomfortable or not important enough for them and did not engage in that activity. I just began to reflect on that, just because I'm comfortable doesn't mean that everybody else is seeing or reading that situation." (Project Manager female C9)

There was also some indication that the use of specific exercises and activities, which were specifically related to the use of emotional intelligence abilities within a project management context, was also associated with supporting greater learning:

"OK one of the biggest things I took from it was kind of, ah, one of those things that is really sort of cathartic, particularly the session on conflict management where we have to think about a situation where we had experienced conflict in the workplace. How it kind of manifested itself, how we coped with it. And that sort of brought up some unexpected memories...Something which I experienced a long time ago in the workplace surfaced and that kind of atmosphere, if you like, seemed to prevail for a lot of people...When we were doing feedback at the end of the session people were like, 'Me, me, I wanna do it, I wanna get this off my chest.' Being in that situation when you are talking about an emotion and how you use and understand and control emotions kind of frees things up. The language I suppose, gives you that permission to speak quite openly and honestly. That was one of the most valuable aspects for me." (Project Manager male A1)

"On the course, three of us had to imagine a difficult scenario to give somebody a very difficult message about something and I had to do that a couple of times recently...I often have to give very uncomfortable messages to people, so it was drawing on those particular skills...It was dealing with a [project member] who was very angry on a number of different levels about a number of different things and highly critical of things, and I actually chose to say nothing. It was a judgment—a judicious choice to say nothing and just let him speak and not interrupt him. What I chose to do was listen very carefully to his feelings and I reflected his feelings back to him. I couldn't promise him anything because it wasn't really in my power. It was all issues relating to things at a much higher level, beyond my limit, so there's no good [in] me saying well you know I can do this for you...So I just listened to the issues and tried my hardest to pick up the feelings and reflect those feelings back to him, and that actually helped, you know...and that was quite powerful. I mean at the end he said I'm not angry with you, you're doing a very good job—that's not the issue here—there are much bigger issues. It was actually about being in control." (Project Manager female B11)

Of significance, a number of participants also suggested that EI development was likely to be an ongoing process and that the impact of training on its own was likely to be limited:

"[With] EI, you don't just leap in and suddenly you are an expert. It's a lifetime work and so the EI course, it's a 2-day thing…It's not just something fresh to me, it's something I've been working on my whole life, personal life, and working life, so you can't learn enough about it. I think it's so important. It helps me to understand what goes wrong in workplaces and in families and in personal relationships. Mostly you are just not enough aware of it yourself." (Project Manager female C7)

"I think in a way you might have sowed seeds. I don't think 2 days can be quite enough to have a kind of an epiphany. But you know, seeds have gone in and I notice these ideas in everything else that I do. I then start thinking about and using the ideas relating to feelings…using them as a tool. Something additional, certainly when it comes to just being in a team, managing a team, seeing how the team operates. Even advising how things could work much better by bringing these things in the open. It's the invisible aspect of work." (Project Manager male A5)

Relevant to this were the comments by a number of project managers that the wider social environment influenced how and if emotional abilities were used. The training had offered an opportunity for these individuals to focus on their own approach to dealing with emotions at work and within projects, and how this was also influenced by the organizational field of which they were a part:

"Ironically, I think the [organization], it's quite dead. It's very flat emotionally. The new team…seems to really acknowledge how people feel. But I think in the [organization], they're really bad at dealing with negative emotions. That's one thing that I've learnt recently from my own experience, but even people at more senior level here they're really reluctant to face difficult situations. One of my colleagues either exploits it or it is swept under the carpet. It's either a complete disaster or just ignored so there's no middle ground for dealing with situation. [The training] really has got me thinking about that." (Project Manager male A8)

"I think it was particularly about the organizational review we are facing at the moment, how the organization is behaving around trust, and how the employer/employee relationship is maintained…I think that trust is quite shaky here and it has an emotional impact." (Project Manager male A1)

"Well, I guess I had a few conversations with people. I think a couple had been about how there seems to be a lack of emotional intelligence here and I guess even a lack of emotional awareness. Many people, they are aware, they just don't really care. It's quite hard to know sometimes…Can you even teach EI or is it something that you just bring more into focus, rather than someone who just has no knowledge of their actions and their impact...which they might use to perhaps better their own behavior towards other people. I know how hard I find it and I think I'm reasonable, but I noticed sometimes just how markedly wrong I got things. On one occasion I think 'oh no, I totally misjudged something.' How could I have got it so wrong? So I think, I guess [the training] has certainly given me something very solid on which to base my thinking...but I don't think people are really willing to discuss their personal feelings. Perhaps it's too much—they are not willing to give that much of themselves away. Which is another symptom here, that emotions can't be shared, they're too dangerous." (Project Manager male A5)

4.6 Discussion

Findings from both the quantitative and qualitative data suggest that the ability, understanding emotions, can be developed in project managers as a result of a 2-day training intervention. Importantly, however, the results suggest that this took place over the 6 months following training. Although based on a subset of the total number of training participants, the data analyses found no statistically significant changes in this emotional ability 1 month following attendance on the training program. Changes were, however, detected 6 months following training in the larger data set. Although not conclusive, the results are strongly suggestive that, whereas training may offer a platform to begin developing this specific emotional ability, additional factors subsequently play a role. The qualitative data offered some insights as to the additional processes that might be implicated. Analysis of the interview data suggested that following attendance on training, many project managers were more consciously aware of trying to understand and anticipate the emotional impact of behaviors and situations within a project management context. For some, this seemed to indicate that they were more intensively cognitively processing emotional information than they had been aware of previously. The considerable range of emotional scenarios and challenges arising from working in their teams and projects, appear to offer rich opportunities for these trainees to put their ability relating to understanding emotions in practice. The additional processes of problem-solving and reflection, associated with experiential learning on the job following training, appear to play a major role in enabling this emotional ability to develop further. This is very much in line with Clarke's (2006a) proposition that emotional abilities may develop through workplace learning methods as a result of "emotional knowledge work."

Related to this, a further major finding to emerge from the qualitative data was the impact of training in increasing the motivation of participants to use their emotional intelligence abilities. A number of participants suggested that they directed more effort and attention following training to considering the emotional nature of working in projects and teams. The role of training in improving participants' motivation to use knowledge and skills has been recognized for some time within the organizational/industrial psychology literature (Colquitt, LePine,

& Noe, 2000; Tannenbaum, Mathieu, Salas, & Canon-Bowers, 1991). Furthermore, that performance is a function of both ability and motivation is also widely accepted (Porter & Lawler, 1968). This would seem to suggest, then, that training programs of short duration such as the one evaluated here, may not only provide initial self-awareness of emotional abilities important to facilitate their future development, but also may impact on participants' EI performance overall, through increasing their motivation to use their existing emotional abilities. This may be a result of increases in trainees' self-efficacy related to the use of their emotional intelligence abilities gained while on the training program. Self-efficacy refers to one's belief in one's capacity to cope with external demands and mobilize the physical, cognitive, and emotional resources needed to succeed in a particular task (Bandura, 1986). Previously, self-efficacy beliefs have been found to be associated with performance across a wide range of task behaviors (Frayne & Latham, 1987; Gist, 1987) and capable of development through training interventions (Gist, Schwoerer & Rosen, 1989). Bandura (1986) has previously identified the major sources of information that strengthen self-efficacy as arising from enactive attainment, vicarious experience, verbal persuasion, and emotional states. Enactive attainment refers to enhancing skills and abilities through practice and feedback, while vicarious experience refers to learning through observation and modeling. Opportunities for participating in structured practice sessions that required participants to consider how emotional abilities may be used in their roles as project managers, practice EI associated behaviors, and then receive feedback were identified by participants as key factors associated with the effectiveness of the training program. This would seem to correspond to learning through enactive attainment. Observing others during role plays also promoted vicarious learning. These are precisely the type of activities which would be expected then to provide information that would lead to strengthening these trainees' levels of self-efficacy in EI-related areas.

Previously, Dulewciz, and Higgs (2004) presented findings using their EIQ measure of emotional intelligence, suggesting that emotional intelligence is capable of development, based upon a sample of 14 team leaders who took part in continuous development exercises (with 13 of them participating in a control group). Using a pre/post-test design with the second set of measures collected 12 months later, they found no differences in the overall EIQ score, or on six of the elements, but did find that conscientiousness had improved. Their EIQ measure contains four key dimensions containing seven subscales which they label as drivers (motivation), constrainers (conscientiousness), intrapersonal enablers (self-awareness, emotional resilience, and intuitiveness), and interpersonal enablers (interpersonal sensitivity and influence). They recognize that some dimensions are likely to be relatively fixed as they represent aspects of personality; however, they suggest that driver and constrainer dimensions are "exploitable" which will impact on the above enablers. These authors concede that the development part of emotional intelligence in their model may well be in the associated motivational aspects rather than in any other areas. The impact of the training in increasing trainees' motivation suggested here would seem to lend some support for this. This might suggest that one of the key benefits of short course training in EI is that it can improve EI performance through its impact on trainees' motivation. However, findings from this study also suggest that there is also scope for actual emotional abilities themselves to be developed. It may be that the combination of increasing awareness of emotional intelligence abilities, increasing trainees' self-efficacy, and enhancing motivation more generally, are all key factors that support the ongoing development of some aspects of emotional intelligence subsequent to attending training through on-the-job learning mechanisms.

The failure to detect any changes in the two emotional abilities of perceiving emotions and using emotions to facilitate thinking was unexpected and contrary to that hypothesized. In relation to the ability of perceiving emotions, Elfenbein (2006) had previously found positive changes in emotion accuracy recognition as a result of a training intervention using an emotion in faces test. Although using a computer-mediated test in order to assess changes in emotional accuracy rather than measuring the emotional ability itself, the study does suggest, nonetheless, that this ability is susceptible to development. In the training program evaluated here, the content focused on emotional recognition more broadly within nonverbal communication, which although it included facial display, it was far wider in its scope looking at kinesthetics, paralanguage, and proxemics (Furnham, 1999; Lyle, 1997). The qualitative data suggest that participants had gained an increased awareness of both of these abilities and were using them in the context of their roles as project managers. One explanation for the failure to find any positive changes in the emotional ability, perceiving emotions, may be that the content of training was not sufficiently matched to the content domain covered in the emotional intelligence test administered. Alternatively, it could be that the half day allocated on the training to develop this emotional ability was insufficient for the trainees to gain increased mastery in this area, such that increases in actual ability following training were not forthcoming.

Previously, Clarke (2007b) found positive effects for the impact of a 1-day emotional intelligence training session followed by a 14-week team-based learning intervention on the ability of using emotions to facilitate thinking. There is some support then, for the notion that this ability is amenable to development through a combination of both training and team learning. Findings from the qualitative data here also suggested that participants were actively using this ability in the course of their experience in teams and projects following attendance on the training. The failure to find any statistically significant changes after 6 months is therefore surprising. A major factor here could lie with the low reliabilities found for the measure of this ability in the study. These were very low, with coefficient alphas of a mere 0.62 pretraining and 0.57 6-months, post-training. A major problem is that few studies using the MSCEIT have reported reliabilities they obtained for each of the individual ability branches. Instead they have often merely referred to those previously obtained by Mayer and Salovey (1997). The extent to which the low reliability obtained here is indicative of a wider problem with this measure is therefore unknown. A further factor is that few studies have used the MSCEIT in field as opposed to experimental settings. It is possible that differing testing conditions may have influenced the reliability of this scale.

It should also be noted that major problems were encountered in the study with respect to attrition among the study population. Follow-up communications with those failing to complete tests indicated that the length of time to complete the emotional intelligence ability test deterred individuals, and it was often difficult for them to fit in the test within the allotted timeframes given their busy work schedules. This could suggest, then, that differing test conditions may cause problems in how individuals respond to particular test items associated with this emotional intelligence ability.

The study also found statistically significant improvements in the self-assessed project management competences of teamwork and managing conflict. It is tempting to assume that the increase in the emotional ability, understanding emotions, may have been associated with all these improvements. In the previous study reported earlier, the emotional intelligence ability, using emotions to facilitate thinking, was found to be associated with the project management competence of teamwork, while the total EI score was positively associated with the competence of managing conflict. It could be that improvements found here in the emotional ability of understanding emotions is also associated with these competences, but the sample size may have precluded detecting a statistically significant result. Arguably, then, improvement in this self-assessed competence could have been the result of underlying improvements in this emotional ability following attendance on training. An alternative explanation may however be that self-ratings in these competence domains increased due to changes in the project managers' motivation. The qualitative data suggest that during the 6 months following training, participants were more motivated to use their emotional abilities. This increase in motivation may have generated further self-efficacy information in these competence areas. Improvements in these project management competences could therefore be due to increases in trainees' self-efficacy beliefs. This being the case, increases in these self-assessment ratings could arguably be due to real changes in actual performance of these competences. In the absence of objective measures of competence, it is clearly difficult in drawing any firm conclusions.

Finally, some mention should be made of the finding obtained here that changes in empathy scores between pre- and 6 months post-training were found to be statistically significant, but had actually decreased over the 6-month period following training. This was in the opposite direction to that hypothesized. Previously, a number of studies had reported positive effects for education and training programs on empathy measures, in a wide range of populations including medical students (Pacala, Boult, Bland, & O'Brien, 1995), nurses (Herbeck & Yammarino, 1990), parents (Brems, Baldwin, & Baxter, 1993) and social work students (Erera, 1997). Similar to many of these other training programs, the activities contained in this training program targeting participants' empathy was underpinned by the work of Goldstein and Michaels (1985). However, a close inspection of these activities would suggest that these activities are more likely to target cognitive dimensions of empathy rather than its emotional dimensions. There is now increasing acceptance that empathy is best viewed as a multidisciplinary construct containing both cognitive and affective dimensions (Davis, 1983; Duan & Hill, 1996). The former, for example, includes cognitive processes such as perspective taking, which involves taking on the perspective of another persons' state of mind without experiencing that person's feelings. The affective component includes dimensions, such as empathic concern, which refers to a dispositional tendency to experience sympathy, compassion, and concern for others, and personal distress, which refers to individual tendencies to respond to distress in others with increased distress in themselves. Shapiro, Morrison, and Boker (2004) have previously suggested that exposure to standardized, cognitive-behavioral methods of instruction appear to have limited impact on developing emotional empathy among medical students. The failure to detect any improvements in empathy here may have been due to the training content more closely associated with cognitive aspects of the empathy construct, while the actual measure of empathy used in the study taps predominantly these latter two emotional dimensions (Kim & Prohner, 2003).

However, this would not explain the statistically significant decrease in affective empathy scores among participants following training. An alternative explanation could be that decreases in emotional empathy were linked to the significant improvements found in the ability, understanding emotions, as a result of the training. Previously Cliffordson (2002) investigated relationships between a multidimensional measure of empathy (the Interpersonal Reactivity Index, IRI [Davis, 1983]) and social skills. The IRI contains four dimensions of empathy: empathic concern, perspective taking, fantasy, and personal distress. In a study involving 127 applicants for nursing and social work degree programs, she found that the PD aspect of emotional empathy was negatively related to the emotional and social control dimensions found in measures of both the IRI and the social skills inventory (SSI, Riggio 1986). The ability of understanding emotions, enables individuals to identify what circumstances cause different emotional responses and how more simple emotions blend to cause more complex emotional states. This knowledge is thought to be important in enabling individuals to understand why they may be experiencing particular feelings, which is prerequisite for considering how these feelings may be best managed or controlled. Improvements in this ability may have assisted trainees to moderate the levels of emotional distress they experienced in response to those items suggesting personal distress in the affective empathy scale used in the study. This does offer a plausible explanation for the statistically significant decrease found in emotional empathy and offers additional support for the training having had some impact on the development of this emotional intelligence ability.

Finally, in addition to factors associated with the design of the training program, the qualitative data also offered some insights into additional factors that may exert significant influences on the development of emotional intelligence abilities. Notably, here a number of trainees indicated that the wider social environment in which they operated may play a role. A number of authors have suggested that it is the level of emotional intelligence at the team level that is important in relation to its influence on teamwork processes and team performance (Druskat & Wolff, 2001; Jordan et al., 2002). Based on social information processing theory (Salancik & Pfeffer, 1978) individuals' attitudes are partially determined by those in their closest proximity, particularly the behavior of co-workers. Attitudes towards performing particular behaviors combined with perceptions of social pressures of whether to perform the behavior (subjective norms) can help to predict the likelihood of that behavior occurring (Azjen, 1981; Fishbein & Azjen, 1975). It would seem likely that an individual's motivation to use their emotional intelligence abilities may very well be influenced by the particular behavioral norms which operate in their immediate environment. Elsewhere team leaders have been suggested as playing a major role in supporting learning and development through attempting to influence group and team norms (Nembhard & Edmondson, 2006). The particular cultural norms and values relating to the extent to which emotions are openly discussed within project environments could therefore feasibly influence opportunities for emotional abilities, such as the ability to understand emotions, to develop. This would correspond with those authors who have argued that organizations should seek to promote a workplace environment which supports a more open discussion of emotions alongside the development of emotional norms in order to promote better emotional management (George, 2000).

4.7 Conclusions

This is the first study to appear in the literature that has investigated whether participation in a short training program can affect the development of emotional intelligence abilities. Previously, Clarke (2006a), in his study of hospice workers, indicated that emotional intelligence abilities and competence in using and understanding emotional knowledge, was gained through reflexive practice within the specific context of the workplace. Empirical studies using the ability model of emotional intelligence have suggested that workplace learning gained through participating in teams and projects may offer key means for developing some of these abilities (Clarke, 2007b; Groves, McEnrue, & Shen, 2008; Moriarty & Buckley, 2007). Findings here that suggest that the emotional intelligence ability of understanding emotions can develop in project managers during the 6 months following participation in training, would seem to offer further support for this position. Although significant changes were only found in one branch of emotional intelligence, understanding emotions, its role in enabling individuals to better manage inter-personal relationships would suggest such training is likely to be of major benefit to organizations where interpersonal work is of major importance.

The evaluation has also identified a number of strategies associated with the design of the training program that seem to be implicated in the development of this EI ability. In particular, the use of case scenarios tailored to a project management context, alongside opportunities to practice and receive feedback on skills using emotional abilities, appear to be important. Similarly learning activities that include opportunities for self reflection on personal use of emotional intelligence and observation of others also seem to be helpful.

However, the limitations associated with the research design suggest that any conclusions should only be treated as tentative at this stage. The evaluation was based on a pilot study comprising a sample of only 53 participants. Although such sample sizes are commonly found within the training evaluation literature (Cromwell & Kolb, 2004; Ibbertson & Newell, 1998; Lim & Morris, 2006), they do nonetheless pose problems with increasing dangers of type I errors. The absence of a suitable comparison group also means that maturational factors cannot be ruled out as accounting for the positive results found. The use of self ratings to assess project management competences is a further major limitation of the study, given that self ratings are generally far more lenient than those from observers (Atwater & Yammarino, 1992; Mabe & West, 1982). A further problem concerned the significant participant attrition, which was encountered particularly at 1 month post-training. However, as a pilot study, the findings here are encouraging in suggesting that training interventions using similar content and design to that described here may result in changes in one major EI ability, understanding emotions, and improvements in the performance of other EI abilities through enhanced motivation. Future studies should aim to replicate this study by involving larger populations and using more objective measures of project manager competences. Future research might also examine whether differences in the emotional norms of teams or projects exert any effects on the development of emotional intelligence following attendance on training.

Section 5.0

Implications of Findings, Directions for Future Research, and Overall Conclusions

5.1 Implications of Findings

5.1.1 Significance of Emotional Intelligence and Empathy for Key Project Competences

Findings from study one reported here found that the emotional intelligence ability of using emotions to facilitate thinking was significantly associated with the project manager competence of teamwork. The overall measure of EI was also associated with the project manager competence of managing conflict. In both instances, this was after controlling for both cognitive ability and personality. Despite limitations associated with the use of self-report measures, these findings do point towards emotional intelligence abilities as offering some explanation to account for differences in performance of these specific competences. These measures accounted for a further 7% and 6% of variation in these competences after personality. These contributions are deemed significant, given the wide range of factors potentially associated with performing these competences. However they do need to be placed in context given that, in both instances, personality was found to account for far greater variation in both teamwork (13%) and managing conflict (20%). Previously, Ilarda and Findlay (2007), using a self-report measure of emotional intelligence derived from Mayer et al.'s (1990) four-ability conceptualization of emotional intelligence (the SUEIT: Palmer & Stough, 2001), found that the total EI score accounted for a further 4% variance in the propensity for teamwork, after the 22% they found for personality. Personality differences would, therefore, seem to be far greater predictors for these two competences. It would seem logical to conclude that certainly, in terms of implications for selecting project managers to perform in projects where these competences are a premium, agencies or organizations would do better to screen based on personality differences in the first instance, with emotional intelligence providing a subsidiary mechanism.

However, this is of little help to those organizations considering how best to improve the performance of project managers in these competence areas, given that personality is a relatively stable set of individual characteristics. Instead the finding that emotional intelligence does contribute to both of these competence areas does suggest potential avenues for organizations to consider in terms of implementing developmental strategies for improving these competences possibly through improving the emotional intelligence of project managers. This is where the positive relationships found here between EI and these competences have the greatest significance, given arguments that these emotional intelligence abilities may be susceptible to development through organizationally sponsored interventions (Clarke, 2006a; Wong, Foo, Wang, & Wong, 2007).

The finding that emotional empathy was associated with the project manager competence described here as "attentiveness" is also significant. A number of studies have suggested that empathy is capable of development through training and development interventions (Erera, 1997; Herbeck & Yammarino, 1990), again suggesting that this may offer a further route for improving project managers' competence in this area. Given the emphasis being placed on these behaviors for building strong inter-personal relationships within projects, short-term education and development programs that combine a focus on both emotional intelligence and empathy may result in some clear benefits.

5.1.2 Emotional Intelligence and Transformational Leadership

The study found that the emotional intelligence ability of using emotions to facilitate thinking accounted for a further 4% in variation in both the transformational leadership behaviors of idealized influence and individualized consideration after controlling for both cognitive ability and personality. Again, notwithstanding limitations associated with the study design, these findings are significant in that they join the growing body of findings suggesting that emotional intelligence abilities are closely associated with performing this particular type of leadership behavior (Ashkanasy & Tse, 2000; Leban & Zulauf, 2004) and indeed does make an independent contribution beyond either cognitive ability or personality (c.f. Antonakis, Avolio, & Sivasubramaniam, 2003).

Leadership involves many types of different behaviors and can be understood from a wide range of perspectives (Northouse, 2003); however, it is the close association of transformational leadership with managing change and ambiguity that makes it particularly relevant for projects (Bommer, Rich, & Rubin, 2005; Eisenbach, Watson, & Pillai, 1999). A number of studies, for example, have found this form of leadership to be associated with organizational ambidexterity (Nemanich & Vera, 2009) a concept closely associated with innovation and change, as well as within volatile conditions, such as those within networks and alliances (Waldman &

Yammarino, 1999). To the extent that projects reflect similar conditions, the finding that the emotional ability of using emotions to facilitate thinking is associated with these transformational leadership dimensions again suggests that developing the EI of project managers may offer significant benefits through its potential capacity to improve transformational leadership behaviors.

However, it should be borne in mind that, to date, there have been mixed results regarding the significance of transformational leadership within project contexts. Keller (2006) studied 118 research and development project teams from five firms. He found transformational leadership predicted 1-year-later technical quality, schedule performance, and cost performance; and 5-year-later profitability and speed to market. By contrast, Keegan and Hartog (2004), in their study of project managers who also had line manager responsibilities, found that transformational leadership correlated positively with commitment and motivation in the line team, but there was no significant link within the project team. They suggested that, although the performance of these leadership behaviors were the same in both contexts, their effects appear to be diluted or have less effect in project contexts. Similarly, Strang (2005), in his case study of four project leaders, found that project leadership did not always require strong transformational leadership behavior to produce effective outcomes.

Elsewhere, a number of authors suggested that there may be boundary conditions connected to transformational leadership that is associated with the type of system, goals pursued, and dynamism of the context (Mumford, 2003; Mumford & Licuanan, 2004; Mumford, Scott, Gaddis, & Strange, 2002; Osborn & Marion, 2009; Pawar & Eastman, 1997). Osborn and Marion's (2009) study of transformational leadership in network alliances, for example, offers further support for the notion that leadership within such systems is about creating order from chaos rather than focused on motivation. To the extent that some projects may reflect contexts with greater uncertainty associated with "near-edge chaos," the importance of transformational leadership, and therefore its association with emotional intelligence, may be of less significant.

5.1.3 Developing the Emotional Intelligence Abilities of Project Managers

This study found support for the positive impact of a 2-day training program on the emotional intelligence ability of understanding emotions in a sample of 53 UK project managers 6 months following attendance on training. This relates to an individual's understanding of how different situations, behaviors, and events can give rise to particular emotional responses in themselves and in others (Mayer & Salovey, 1997). This ability has been suggested as important in work contexts as emotional knowledge of this kind can assist individuals to better negotiate social encounters and to use this knowledge in the proactive building of interpersonal relationships (Lopes et al., 2003, 2004). It has also been suggested as important in leadership contexts for knowing when and how to use effect in order to stimulate creativity, optimism, and generate excitement among followers in the pursuit of goals (George, 2000; Prati et al., 2003). Emotions play a significant role in shaping attitudes and behaviors at work (Weiss & Cropanzano, 1996). A knowledge of how different emotions are generated and how they can influence attitudes and behaviors is likely to offer project managers distinct advantages within contexts where they are dependent on building commitment and trust rapidly in order for individuals to work effectively together within project contexts (Bresnen & Marshall, 2000; Burgess & Turner, 2000; Hartman, 2000). However, the results suggest that the impact of training on this ability may not be seen immediately and it is likely to be some months before any improvements can be detected. It may be that although training can provide an initial self-awareness of the importance of emotions, the actual processes associated with its development continue taking place after training through on-the-job learning mechanisms (Clarke, 2006a). This would seem to correspond with other studies that have found developments in ability-derived measures of EI within team learning contexts (Clarke, 2007b; Groves, McEnrue & Shen, 2006; Moriarty & Buckley, 2003).

5.1.4 Improving the Performance of Emotional Intelligence Abilities of Project Managers

A further finding from the evaluation of the training program is that training can impact in two ways. The first as described previously, is its potential to serve as a basis for further development of particular EI abilities. The second major impact is its potential for improving the motivation of trainees to use their existing abilities that comprise emotional intelligence. Given that performance comprises both ability and motivation components (Porter & Lawler, 1968), this in itself is a major benefit of attending training such as that described here. Previous research has suggested that the effects of EI on performance may well be more indirect than direct in nature, such that individuals must not only have EI abilities, but they must be motivated to use them (Rode et al., 2007). It is feasible then that improvements in EI-related performance may be found not as a result of improvements in EI abilities, but through improving the motivation of project managers to use these specific abilities. This in itself may be sufficient reason to invest in training programs, even if actual abilities themselves are not found to improve.

5.1.5 Considerations for Designing Emotional Intelligence Ability—Development Interventions

The findings from the study suggest that, as far developing the emotional intelligence ability of understanding emotions is concerned, organizations wishing to develop project managers' abilities in this area might achieve similar positive results if they adopt identical strategies to the design of the training program to those outlined here. Key aspects associated with the design of the training program included: (1) opportunities for participating in structured practice sessions that required participants to consider how emotional abilities may be used in their roles as project managers; (2) practicing EI-associated behaviors and then receiving feedback; and (3) observing others during role plays and simulations. The use of these specific development strategies promote learning and strengthen self-efficacy (Bandura, 1986).

However, factors outside the training program itself may also exert some effects that potentially influence whether EI abilities may develop, once trainees return on the job. In particular, the wider social environment is likely to impact on opportunities that are available for trainees to discuss and subsequently use emotional information, which feasibly might also influence subsequent EI ability development. A major factor may be the characteristics of emotionally competent group norms (Druskat & Wolff, 2001) associated with either the organizational culture or project contexts which could place limitations or constraints on opportunities for further EI development (Clarke, 2006a). This would suggest that wherever possible, EI development activities are best undertaken with individuals based within the same teams or working together in the same project, in order to maximize opportunities for developing appropriate group norms to support ongoing EI development.

5.1.6 Impact of Emotional Intelligence Training on Project Manager Competences and Performance

There have been criticisms of competence-based approaches to defining the professional body of knowledge necessary for project management (Ruuska & Vartiainen, 2003). For many, these criticisms mirror those which can be found more widely in the management literature generally (Johnson, Lorenz, & Lundrall, 2002; Lewis, 1998; Roger & Philip, 1997), in that competences tend to adopt a reductionist approach to defining the knowledge base that may be required for effective project management. Supporting this view are a number of studies that show, despite a growing body of knowledge, its effective implementation can be highly problematic (Williams, 1999, 2005). Although this draws attention to questions of implementation and is perhaps an insufficient argument in itself for challenging their utility (Crawford, 2005; El-Sabaa, 2001), this does, nonetheless, draw attention to the extent to which project management has tended to adopt overly rationalistic and functionalist perspectives in understanding the roles and work undertaken or enacted within project management.

Ruuska and Vartiainen (2003) argue for the need to recognize the notion of collective competences that are the property of the project management team. Based upon a situated learning perspective (e.g., Lave & Wenger, 1991), this approach recognizes how explicit knowledge, as represented by a set of professional management competences, fails to sufficiently address the procedural or tacit knowledge that project managers need to carry out their work or implement their knowledge. This inevitably draws attention to the specific context in which project managers are operating, as exerting a significant influence on how they carry out their tasks (or implement their knowledge). A significant component of this context is the social network or relational field surrounding the project manager, which will affect how they are able to obtain, share, and interpret the knowledge they rely on for achieving project success. Given such considerations, any expectations that interventions designed to develop emotional intelligence necessarily will result in improvements in these key competence areas may need to be treated with some degree of caution.

However, beyond merely those specific project manager competences examined here, the finding that emotional intelligence abilities can be enhanced and the use of such abilities improved through training, clearly has much wider implications for enhancing project managers' performance. For example, an awareness of others' emotions within projects should help project managers in understanding others' needs and help with team bonding. Such bonding and close interpersonal ties can help build trust, resolve conflict, and promote closer cooperation (Jones & George, 1998; McAllister, 1995). Understanding how events in projects can trigger specific emotional responses that then impact on performance can assist project managers in planning, setting, and communicating tasks (Jordan, Ashkanasy, Hartel, & Hooper 2002). These all represent areas which have been cited in the literature as key elements associated with successful outcomes in projects (Kerzner, 2001; Lester, 1998; Munns & Bjeirmi, 1996; Pinto & Slevin, 1988; Randolph & Posner, 1988; Taborda, 2000). Elsewhere, it has also been found that positive effect among construction project managers was a key factor associated with their coping and adjustment to dealing with stress, thereby avoiding psychological problems (Haynes & Love, 2004). Beyond project effectiveness, it would seem likely that there may well be other major gains that could be made in terms of wider health and well-being factors of those involved in projects. Together these suggest a rich vein of further research to identify the various ways in which emotional intelligence might impact projects.

5.2 Directions for Future Research

The findings from these two pilot research studies examining emotional intelligence in projects suggest that (1) EI abilities and empathy have additional explanatory power to predict project manager's competence in the areas of teamwork, attentiveness, and managing conflict, as well as in the transformational leadership dimensions of idealized influence and individualized consideration; and (2) training seems to have a positive impact on the development and use of emotional intelligence by project managers. Based on these findings, further research seems warranted that use more robust methodologies in order to confirm the significant relationships found here. Firstly, the use of self-report measures of project manager competences is a limitation of this research that future studies should seek to improve upon. The use of supervisor ratings of performance in these areas can provide more valid measures. However, more objective means for measuring the project manager competences of teamwork, attentiveness, and conflict management would be preferable in order to confirm the relationships between emotional intelligence abilities, empathy, and these particular competences. Previous studies in conflict management, for example, have assessed this competence through video-taped performance simulations which could be adapted for project management contexts (Maher, 1986; Webster-Stratton & Hammond, 1999). Similarly, in relation to transformational leadership, the use of ratings from others involved in a project combined with supervisory ratings would offer an advance on the methodology employed here.

Next, although it is intuitive to consider that differences in emotional abilities may account for variations in particular project manager competences, it is possible that proficiency in such competences could lead to these emotional intelligence abilities being enhanced. Future studies that employ a longitudinal design may reveal insights into the direction of causality here. In addition to strengthening the methodological approach of assessing project manager competences and transformational leadership, future studies should also seek to identify whether the significant relationships found here can be replicated using much larger populations. This will increase the power of statistical tests to detect relationships. There is also a need to identify whether emotional intelligence abilities are associated with other key project manager behaviors associated with successful project outcomes. In particular, the use of current items of competence, drawn from the PMI *Project Manager Competency Development Framework* (PMI, 2007) relating to communication, were found to be far too broad in scope to be used to underpin a satisfactory measure of communication, which might be expected to be associated with emotional intelligence. Future research should therefore make use of other measures available in the literature that could more effectively capture emotional and social communication in order to determine relationships here.

There is also a need to identify more clearly the extent to which the project manager behaviors, thought to be associated with project effectiveness and associated with emotional intelligence abilities, actually account for variations in project outcomes. This should involve researchers specifying a priori, which specific project manager competences or behaviors are likely to be more important within differing project contexts. A major area of research here involves identifying how differences in managing change, complexity, and ambiguity may be defining features which affect the relative influence of emotional intelligence. Given empirical findings elsewhere, suggesting that emotional intelligence may differentiate how individuals manage change (Higgs & Rowland, 2002; Groves, 2006) and theoretical propositions suggesting that emotional intelligence may influence how individuals respond to change (George & Jones, 2001; Huy, 1999, 2002), this would seem to warrant further research.

There is also far more research needed to examine the impact of training and development interventions specifically on emotional intelligence abilities. Again, future studies should attempt to determine whether the positive effects found here for attendance on EI training can be replicated using larger samples. Findings from this research have suggested that training results in the actual development of one of the four emotional abilities which forms part of the EI ability model, that relating to understanding emotions. This may have been due to the focus and content of the training where there was considerable emphasis in this emotional ability domain. It may be that short-duration training programs, such as the one described here which are more clearly targeted towards one emotional ability, may offer a greater chance of success, as opposed to those which seek to address all four abilities within such short durations. Future research should therefore investigate the extent to which training targeted to individual emotional abilities is effective. Based on qualitative data, the evaluation here also suggested that training may result in improvements in EI ability performance, due to its impact on project managers' self-efficacy and motivation. Future studies should specifically investigate the impact of EI training on performance by including measures of self-efficacy to provide greater insights into its potential role here. Finally, there is a need to devise future studies which enable us to better understand the mechanisms by which emotional intelligence abilities potentially develop. Findings here suggested that actual development occurred during the 6 months after participants had attended training. This does suggest that there are additional factors outside training itself which play a significant role on EI development. Clarke (2006a) suggested that this may involve a number of processes associated with workplace or on-the-job learning. Future studies should therefore examine the post-training environment focusing on areas such as the nature of project learning climates, including opportunities for reflection and dialogue which relate to emotional experiences in projects. The nature of group norms that may influence how open project members are to addressing emotional information, as well as the intensity of emotional experiences on projects, are also fruitful areas to investigate that might reveal additional insights here.

5.3 Overall Conclusions

The behavioral dimensions of project management have increasingly moved from being seen as peripheral to now a far wider recognition of their central importance to the effectiveness of projects. Traditional approaches to project management, with its emphasis on rationality and planning, have generally ignored the extent to which projects as social and relational systems are major sources of emotion which influences the attitudes, cognitions, decisions, and behaviors of all those involved. Emotional intelligence is an aspect of individual difference that is associated with differences in how people identify, use, understand, and manage emotions that have been found to be associated with a wide range of important personal and work-related outcomes. Included in the latter have been areas such as communication, teamwork, managing conflict, and leadership. Projects represent newer forms of work organization, which have been suggested among other things to place particular emphasis on individuals' abilities to manage complexity and ambiguity, form strong interpersonal relationships within relatively short spaces of time, and successfully manage conflict situations that are more likely to arise given the nature of such work systems. Emotional intelligence is widely thought by many to potentially offer distinct advantages for individuals working within projects, given findings from wider research. To date, however, there have been relatively few studies that have specifically investigated emotional intelligence within project contexts. Although a number of these have shown some promising results, there are significant limitations due to problems associated with the way in which emotional intelligence has been measured in these studies and the failure to control for both general mental ability and personality, which make it difficult to draw satisfactory conclusions regarding the actual impact of emotional intelligence in these areas.

This pilot research involved two studies that sought to further our understanding of the role emotional intelligence may play specifically within project contexts by using a measure of emotional intelligence that has received the most support within the literature as capturing a unique and distinct area of individual difference. The first study found significant relationships between emotional intelligence ability measures and empathy with the project manager competences of teamwork, managing conflict, and attentiveness. The second study found positive effects for participation in a 2-day EI training program 6 months later on the emotional intelligence ability of understanding emotions. The results from the qualitative data also suggested that the training may well have impacted on EI performance more generally through increasing the self-efficacy and motivation of trainees. Notwithstanding, limitations associated with the approach used to measure project manager competences in the study, the findings from this pilot research provide further support for the growing literature, which suggests that emotional intelligence may be of particular significance for working in and managing projects. Of major significance, the positive results found for the impact of training suggest that the utility of the emotional intelligence concept for projects is not merely limited to considerations of selecting individuals that may perform more effectively where such competences are deemed a premium. Instead, the results suggest that organizations could improve project manager competences in these specific areas through development interventions that are designed to target emotional intelligence. The results from this pilot research suggest that further research studies in project contexts using the ability-derived construct of emotional intelligence may offer further insights into understanding individual factors that may be associated with the effectiveness of projects.

SECTION 6.0

Developing Emotional Intelligence Training: Theoretical and Empirical Underpinnings

To date, developing an emotional intelligence (EI) training program based upon the evaluation studies presents a number of challenges, not least due to the limited data available regarding those factors associated with the design of these programs that may have been associated with their effectiveness. The following details the chief considerations and theoretical insights that were drawn upon to inform the development of the EI training program evaluated here.

6.1 The Duration of Programs

The first challenge in designing an appropriate EI training program concerns the optimal duration of training, which is likely to then result in some favorable impact. A major problem here is that of the seven EI training and development studies thus far available in the literature, only four of these were actually designed to target EI abilities as opposed to other EI models. Furthermore, all but one of these studies were based on student populations with the program delivered in an educational setting. Issues of generalizability, beyond student populations to workers in organizational settings, are therefore an issue. Furthermore, attempting to isolate these design factors, which may have contributed to improvements in emotional intelligence from educational programs, presents particular challenges. For example, Moriarty and Buckley (2003) describe a program that took place 2 hours per week over 12 weeks, plus additional weekly team meetings. Groves, McEnrue, and Shen (2008) describe an 11-week course, although the cumulative time involved in sessions is not specified. Clarke (2007b), by contrast, outlined a 14-week course, which consisted of a 1-day specific EI training session followed by teams meeting on a project-based activity over the 14-week period. The only three programs reported, which were targeted at those in actual work settings, reported durations of training programs ranging from a few days for dentists and their administrative staff (Meyer et al., 2004), to a 5-day course over 5 weeks for retail managers (Slaski & Cartwight, 2003). Elsewhere, EI training courses for employees have also been reported as being effective after 4 or 5 days, divided into two segments separated by 1 or 2 months (www.eiconsortium.org). Although there is no definitive answer to the optimal duration of a training program, the only message one can draw with any certainty here is that it does seem clear that participants require a period of time with which to embed any new learning and to practice developing their emotional competences or abilities. This would seem to suggest that although training programs can offer a platform from which to begin the development of emotional intelligence, there is likely to be some time delay before any significant change or improvements are realized.

6.2 The Content: Developing Self-Awareness

There were a number of more general aspects of how these programs were structured and designed, from which certain factors could be identified, that may have been associated with their effectiveness. The extent to which these figured in most of the studies evaluated that did show some positive results does give a strong indication that these factors may be significant.

6.2.1 Understanding the Concept of EI

A clear and consistent message that can be drawn from most of the studies evaluated was, that in every instance, there was a sustained focus on developing self-awareness of emotional intelligence and either the abilities or competences that comprise it. Each program began with imparting information on the model of emotional intelligence that underpinned the program and identifying the significance of emotional intelligence for understanding behavior and interpersonal relationships.

6.2.2 Awareness of One's Own Emotional Intelligence Strengths and Weaknesses

A further consistent feature of most training programs evaluated to date was that participants either received insights into or feedback on their own emotional abilities or competences. In some instances, this began with feedback on the results of any EI test that had been undertaken which was seen as an integral part of beginning the process for potential development. Depending upon the model of emotional intelligence underpinning the program, participants then engaged in a range of activities and exercises designed to enable them to receive real-time feedback on differing aspects of their emotional intelligence. In two studies, there appeared to be a specific focus on recognizing emotional display (Clarke, 2007b; Slaski & Cartwiright, 2003). Elfenbein (2003) has provided empirical support for the impact that training can have in improving this emotional ability and identified how through practice, trainees can improve the accuracy with which they recognize displays of emotion through both facial display and other forms of nonverbal behavior. In a number of these programs, there were also exercises provided on how to better regulate emotions and consider the impact of emotions on others (Clarke, 2007b; Slaski & Cartwright, 2003), in one instance, with a focus on conflict management (Moriarty & Buckley, 2003).

6.2.3 Learning Methods

A number of these studies also reported the frequent use of three-learning methods, in particular those that were used to support the development of training participants' self-awareness of emotional intelligence. The first study used structured exercises in order to provide participants' insights into aspects of their interpersonal behavior or preferences. In two studies, there was a specific focus on examining individuals' emotional responses to situations and how emotions then impact on their own and others' behaviors (Slaski & Cartwright, 2003; Clarke, 2007b). A focus on effective teamwork behaviors in two studies was also used to examine the emotional dimensions of behavior (Moriarty & Buckley, 2003; Groves et al., 2008). In addition, there was extensive use made of simulations and role plays in order for participants to demonstrate or practice emotional abilities or competences, and where they received feedback on these, either from other participants or a facilitator. Finally in some instances, there was mention made of a coaching element as a key feature of these programs, where participants received ongoing feedback on their own abilities and areas for personal improvement during the actual development intervention (Groves et al., 2003; Slaski & Cartwright, 2003; Moriarty & Buckley, 2003).

6.3 Designing Emotional Intelligence Training: Drawing From the Wider Literature

There exists a vast literature that has accumulated over the past 50 years that has been drawn upon to underpin the design and delivery of training and development programs (Ford, Kozlowski, Kraiger, Salas, & Teachout, 1997; Goldstein, 1993; Latham, 1988; Quinones & Ehrenstein, 1997). Much of this material is still valid and continues to form the basis for developing many types of training programs, especially those that are concerned with the development of certain types of skills or increasing particular types of knowledge. However, the use of training programs, especially those typically based on behaviorist learning principles as a means to secure learning and change, have been found to be deficient over recent years, as the knowledge and skills required of much of the workforce has increased in complexity. Indeed, studies have continued to highlight the limitations of training programs to often achieve the aims and objectives that were set for them with increasing difficulties encountered in securing the actual transfer of training to use on the job (Clarke, 2001; Ford & Weissbein, 1997). The influence of the work environment to which trainees return, as well as differing job constraints, combine with motivational issues to often impede the success of training (Clarke, 2002, 2006c; Rouillier & Goldstein, 1993;

Tracey, Tannenbaum, & Kavagnah, 1995). Inevitably, this has led to an increasing focus on post-training or follow-up strategies in an attempt to improve the success of training in achieving the improvements that the designers had in mind (Gist, Stevens, & Bavetta, 1991; Marx, 1982; Wexley & Baldwin, 1986). Improvements in the design of training programs, however, have also followed, often with increasing use of experiential learning methods as a means to improve learning and retention on training programs (Kolb, 1985). Nevertheless, critics still point to considerable limitations with such an approach as the best means for supporting learning for use in the workplace (Beckett, 1999; Raelin, 2000).

Specifically, in relation to emotional intelligence training, we are confronted with additional problems which pose further challenges in considering how best to design development interventions. Most typical approaches to the design of training draw upon behaviorist and cognitive theories of learning (Goldstein, 1993; Ford et al., 1997). Typically, there is a focus on breaking complex skills down to smaller skill elements with trainees practicing more elementary skills, receiving feedback to improve performance, and then gradually consolidating learning so as to master more complex skills. Cognitive approaches focus on maximizing trainees' abilities to memorize and retain new information, and attempt to apply novel information to new problems. Cherniss, Goleman, Emmerling, Cowan, and Adler (1998) highlight how the development of social and emotional competences and abilities pose very different challenges for learning since they involve different areas of the brain, and may present very different motivational issues for those engaged in the process. They make a number of key points that highlight a need for learning that engages the emotional centers of the brain. Drawing upon research from fields as diverse as sports psychology, psychotherapy, and personal change, they highlight three points of particular significance:

6.3.1 Emotional Learning Involves Other Areas of the Brain

Some emotional abilities or competences may involve the use of both cognitive and emotional areas of the brain. Although higher cognitive abilities related to information processing are situated in the neocortex, the emotional centers exist elsewhere, particularly in the amygdala, which is located deeper in the brain. The neural pathways that run between these centers develop over a person's lifetime and reflect habitual responses to situations and stimuli that are learned very early on and become difficult to change. The intimate interactions between thought, feelings, and actions become firmly established and supported by the existing network of neural pathways between the emotional and higher cognitive regions of the brain. Attempting to develop emotional abilities that reflect how we process and deal with emotional information requires that we engage these pathways and engage in activities or experiences that provide new insights and alternative solutions, thus extending our response options. This in turn will create further neural circuitry.

This has several implications for the design of emotional intelligence training programs. The most important is the need to engage individuals in experiential activities where they are engaging both these areas of the brain simultaneously. It means considering the inclusion of activities that are likely to generate sufficient emotional content which can form the basis for reflection and discussion. Next, it suggests that individuals need to be involved in exercises or simulations where they are able to receive feedback on how these emotional abilities are put into action so they are able to consider any changes they wish to make. This may take some time and require individuals to engage in critical thinking and reflect on relevant experiences far beyond those provided on a training program. Finally it suggests that there may also be a need for unlearning, if established ways of doing things, such as how one has regulated their emotions or managed impulsive behavior, are found to be in need of change.

6.3.2 Emotional Learning Challenges Issues of Identity

It would seem clear from 6.3.1 that developing emotional competences or abilities involves engaging on a far more personal level with training than many individuals may have done in the past. This raises immediate questions of managing participant expectations of the training and allaying any anxieties it may generate. This is likely to have a significant influence on either participants' motivation to engage in the training in the first place, or how they interact when they are physically present on the training program itself. Effectively preparing participants prior to their attending training would therefore seem important to ensuring that they know what to expect and feel comfortable with the content of the program. Gaining insights into one's emotional competences, which are evidently a far more personal and intimate part of one's persona, necessitates that individuals confront issues about who they are and what information on emotional competence means to them. Therefore, there is a significant emphasis needed for the creation of a safe and supportive environment where participants are able to gain insights into their own emotional abilities without feeling a threat to their self-esteem.

6.3.3 Emotional Learning Requires Insight and Feedback

Chernis et al. (1998) also stress the importance of self-awareness of one's emotional competences as a central part of any EI development program; therefore, activities should be designed to maximize insight and feedback to the individual in these areas. Individuals are mostly less aware of their strengths and weaknesses in these aspects of their abilities, even though they may have more general views as to how well they may perform in social situations or in personal interactions. Providing simulations and role plays that involve participants in demonstrating these competences should offer opportunities for participants to receive feedback on how they may have used their emotional competences; these are powerful mechanisms for providing insight and promoting personal growth. This places a significant emphasis on the need for individuals to provide feedback in a sensitive way to avoid the issue of individuals becoming defensive and, in so doing, closing themselves off from learning. Considering how feedback is given and planning for structured feedback on the program are likely to be of greater benefit to the participants involved and offer more opportunity for motivating change.

6.4 Developing Emotional Intelligence: Insights From Workplace Learning

Beyond the use of training programs to support learning, a considerable body of literature has been built up over the past two decades, in particular, demonstrating the significant advantages offered through learning new knowledge and skills on the job or in the workplace itself, referred to as workplace learning (Boud & Garrick, 1999; Conlon, 2004). Specifically in relation to the development of emotional intelligence, Clarke (2006a) posited a model as to how emotional abilities may develop through workplace learning based upon qualitative data he obtained from a study conducted involving hospices. Importantly, he suggested that emotional abilities can develop as a result of staff day-to-day interactions with their colleagues and supervisors, through a number of key learning mechanisms.

Firstly, he showed that many of these healthcare workers made considerable use of emotional information as part of their work role and that their emotional abilities were particularly enhanced through a process of focused dialogue and reflection. This development centered on their developing greater proficiency as part of increased professionalization in recognizing emotions, using their knowledge of emotions to inform their healthcare practice, and managing their own emotions and also helping others to regulate their emotional responses. Supportive organizational structures that promoted the discussion of emotion and focused on how to manage emotions also influenced development and learning. Clarke labeled this process of developing emotional intelligence abilities through ongoing dialogue with colleagues and peers and structured reflection on the emotional content arising from work as *emotional knowledge work.* There was also an indication that much of this learning may also occur through more tacit or intuitive means, which is often outside the conscious awareness of the learner, but through dialogue and reflection, this learning was brought into a more conscious awareness on the part of the learner. The key elements of the workplace learning model showing how EI abilities develop are shown in Figure 1. The model posits a number of mechanisms by which emotional intelligence abilities potentially develop. The major points are as follows:

(1) Individuals utilize and learn about their emotional abilities in social encounters within the workplace, where they are constantly presented with emotional knowledge as part of their work role. This emotional knowledge is given meaning as individuals negotiate their relationships and the impact of their behaviors specifically within workplace social structures (Lave & Wenger 1991). Over time, they develop greater competence in recognizing the cues that prompt emotional responses and their impact, through participating in opportunities for learning offered by emotional experiences.

(2) This learning occurs when reflection on these emotional experiences takes place alongside dialogue with their colleagues and peers, a process referred to as "emotional knowledge work." Where workplaces have a culture that

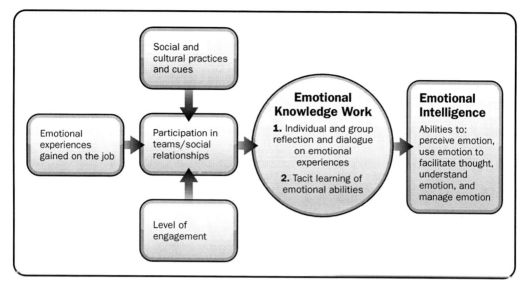

Figure 1. How Emotional Abilities Can Develop Through Workplace learning (based on Clarke (2006b).

supports such reflection and dialogue, in addition to providing opportunities for staff to do so, this offers greater opportunities for emotional intelligence abilities to develop.

(3) Through strengthening social ties within workgroups, individuals enhance their identification with these groups, thereby increasing opportunities for emotional learning and knowledge exchange to occur (Brown & Duguid 1991).

(4) There is also a tacit element associated with the development of emotional intelligence abilities, such that learning and development can also occur outside the conscious awareness of the learner through observation and vicarious learning (Bandura, 1986). Again emotional knowledge work can help in bringing this tacit knowledge to a state of more conscious awareness in learners.

The model recognizes that it is the workplace itself which represents one of the most significant loci for generating emotions in people's lives (Weiss & Cropanzano, 1996), but further explains that social learning within groups, teams, and other key relationships within organizations also provides the means through which the abilities that comprise emotional intelligence might be enhanced. The model also places significant emphasis on the organization's culture in terms of the support it may or may not offer for effectively engaging with the emotional content of work; and this may influence opportunities for EI development. On the basis of this model, training programs would seem to be more limited mechanisms for generating learning opportunities associated with emotional knowledge work and thereby developing emotional intelligence abilities. However, the model does offer a number of insights into how emotional intelligence abilities may develop which can be drawn upon in order to increase the effectiveness of an emotional intelligence training program. These were used to underpin the EI training program evaluated here and were as follows:

(1) *Maximize Real-Life Opportunities for Experiencing Emotions.* Since the development of emotional abilities according to Clarke's model must start with an emotional substrate, activities need to be designed that are able to generate real emotions among training participants. As far as possible, then, cases or situations that form the basis of developmental activities should attempt to integrate or approximate real-life situations involving significant emotional content as far as possible.

(2) *Provide Sufficient Opportunity for Reflection and Dialogue.* Participants need to be offered time to reflect on the emotions generated within scenarios and simulations on training, and to consider how their emotional abilities are being used within these contexts. Facilitating discussions between participants on how they understand and make sense of emotional information should therefore form a key component of the training program in order to support learning and development.

(3) *Focus on Social and Emotional Norms Within the Workplace.* The organizations to which participants belong play a significant part in determining the extent to which emotions and emotional knowledge generated is a source of learning and development dependent upon the social or emotional norms that are present (Wolff & Druskat, 2001). These may either offer pervasive cues that prevent discussion of emotions and their impact, or alternatively these may potentially offer more open and supportive climates that facilitate engagement with how people feel in the organization. Individuals are likely to experience far more restricted opportunities to develop their emotional abilities if, once they return to their workplaces, they return to unsupportive climates. Raising awareness of organizational emotional norms can assist individuals to consider how these might be challenged within their workplace social structures and identify how resources might be mobilized for challenging them.

(4) *Sufficient Time for Development.* One of the key findings from Clarke's (2006a) study of hospice workers indicating how emotional intelligence abilities may develop through workplace learning, was that this development involved some period of time and very much mirrored the workers' sense of increasing professionalization in their work roles. This would strongly suggest that the development of emotional intelligence abilities occurs over a longer time frame than that typically provided on training programs. Training programs might offer a basis for raising awareness of emotional intelligence and initiating the process of EI development. However, it would seem that only through an ongoing and conscious effort on the part of the learner in consciously exercising these emotional abilities may significant improvements or changes eventually take place. Offering training participants clear advice for continuing to exercise these emotional abilities following their

attendance in training should therefore form a key part of the training program. Through trainees attempting more deliberate reflections on how their emotional intelligence may be of use to them in their working lives, the learning process is more likely to continue with positive change and improvement.

6.5 Overview of the Training Program

The 2-day emotional intelligence training program was designed to draw upon the aforementioned principles in order to maximize the opportunity for developing emotional intelligence abilities. A key feature was the design of training materials, exercises, and case simulations that attempted to reflect real-life or actual project management contexts and work challenges. The objectives of the 2-day program and an outline of the 2 days were presented to training participants as follows:

6.5.1 Program Objectives

(1) To facilitate integration of your own personal experiences and thoughts of the emotional dimensions of working in projects with current understanding of the role that emotional intelligence plays in interpersonal behavior.
(2) To enable you to consider your strengths and weaknesses in how you manage the emotional content of project working so as to improve key project management competences.
(3) To assist you in developing emotional abilities that comprise emotional intelligence so as to improve teamwork and leadership behaviors in projects.

6.5.2 Program Overview

6.5.2.1 *Day One Outline:*

9:00–9:15   Welcome, Introductions & Program Overview

9:15–10:15   Emotional Intelligence & Projects Presentation

Here a Powerpoint lecture presentation was given explaining the nature of emotional intelligence, key findings from research, and its relevance for working in and managing projects.

10:15–10:30 Break

10:30–11:30 Emotional Self Awareness: Confessors & Listeners

<u>Exercise/Activity: Exercise 1</u>
The first major exercise of the program focused on examining emotional responses during personal interactions. Participants were asked to form pairs and take turns acting as a listener or confessor (talker) discussing something significant about themselves. The exercise was designed so that one of the listeners during the exercise was purposefully negative or obstructive. All participants discussed

their emotional responses during the exercise in a large plenary group afterwards. Details of the exercise can be found in Appendix 2.

11:30–12:30 Recognizing Emotional Display

Exercise/Activity: Exercise 2
The second exercise of the training program aimed to target improvements in participants' ability to perceive emotions in others. The exercise involved watching a short video clip taken from a well-known movie and then attempting to interpret the meaning and emotions associated with the nonverbal communication and body language that was conveyed in the clip. Details of the exercise can be found in Appendix 3.

12.30–1.30 Lunch

1.30–2.30 Rapport & Empathy

Exercise/Activity: Exercises 3 & 4
The third major exercise focused on communicating emotional understanding through rapport and empathy. This involved two exercises. The first asked participants to consider the content of verbal empathetic messages and how to convey empathy using some simple case vignettes. The second more substantial exercise required participants to form pairs and practise rapport generating behaviors and communicating empathy. Details of the exercise can be found in Appendix 4.

2.30–3.15 Project Case Role Plays

Exercise/Activity: Exercise 5
This substantial exercise in the training program aimed to establish a closer identification between emotional intelligence abilities and the behaviors demonstrated by project managers in project situations. Three case study role plays were developed based on the literature or realistic case scenarios. Each case role play had two roles which were played by a training participant. A third training participant acted as an observer and recorded the personal interaction that took place. The aim of the exercise was for participants to gain insights into their more habitual behaviors that may be socio-emotional positive or socio-emotional negative. Different case role plays were used on each of the three occasions the training program was delivered that were more suited to the work context of the trainees. Details of the exercise and role play material can be found in Appendix 5.

3.15–3.30 Break

3.30–4.30 Project Case Role Plays Continued & Debrief

4.30–5.15   Emotional Climate Exercise

Exercise/Activity: Exercise 6

The final exercise of the first day offered an opportunity for trainees to identify the characteristics of their organizational, work, and project climates that they believed may impact on their using emotionally intelligent behavior. The exercise aimed for delegates to consider the significance of the post-training environment and strategies they might use in order to support the use of emotional intelligence in their roles as project managers. Details of the exercise can be found in Appendix 6.

5.15–5.30   Summary of Day & Debrief

5.30   Close

6.5.2.2 *Day Two Overview:*

The second day was designed to use and apply the information and learning from the first day but with a specific focus on conflict management. The delegates were provided with an overview of conflict styles and strategy and were then were given a process and opportunity to practice engaging in a difficult conversation.

9.00–9.15   Tea/Coffee

9.15–9.30   Welcome, Introductions & Overview of Day

9.30–9.45   Video of Group Exercise: Working together as a team to make a perfect square with a rope

Exercise/Activity

The important thing about this exercise was that there was as little explanation as possible—the understanding was by doing. The exercise required that the group form a circle. Each participant was required to wear a blindfold (blindfolds were   placed on the chair of each participant). The participants were told to make a shape with the rope placed in the centre (square or circle). They were given four minutes to complete the task.

9.45–10.30   Emotional Intelligence in Projects: Large Group Exercise
              What Does Emotionally Intelligent Behavior Look Like in Project Managers?

Exercise /Activity

The first exercise was a large group exercise that asked participants to brainstorm what they considered emotionally intelligent behavior looked like in projects. Individuals were asked to suggest specific behaviors that they thought were underpinned by high emotional intelligence and these were recorded on a flip chart by the facilitator. The aim of the exercise was to develop a greater understanding of how emotional intelligence was used by project managers using specific work examples generated by participants.

10:30–10.45 Break

10.45–1.00   The Nature of Conflict in Projects and Personal Conflict Handling Styles

Exercise/Activity
At this stage it was felt necessary to communicate to the group that conflict was inevitable and normalized the appearance of conflict in the workplace. Understandably when people think of conflict, they may think of it in a variety of different ways. So, one of the best ways to get some understanding is to ask the group. The group was asked to write down the first thing that they thought of when thinking about conflict. They were then asked to share with the group their thoughts and these were then recorded. Then, as a group, they worked through the definition of conflict (as defined by CEDR).

Conflict – Constructive/Destructive
The earlier discussion revealed that conflict was often considered to be more negative and that people try to avoid engaging in conflict. However, there are occasions where conflict is necessary to ensure the success of a project and it provides some additional assistance to the effective functioning of a project team.

Different types of conflict were introduced:
• Task conflict—what should be done?
• Process conflict—how should we do the task?
• Relationship conflict—who should do what? How should they interact?

Once individuals realized that conflict was something that could be managed, then they should have been more willing to deal with it proactively. This brought in the concept of proportional conflict composition, the idea that there should be a certain amount of conflict; timing is key to the perception of conflict as being either positive or negative.

For example: A project is assigned to a team—what should they do to minimize conflict?
• *Process conflict*—At the beginning of a project there will be moderately high levels of process conflict (work is agreed upon, deadlines set, responsibilities are established); however, this will diminish as the project continues and will increase again as the project comes to completion.
• *Task conflict*—At the beginning of a project there should be a fairly low level of task conflict (otherwise it will interfere with procedural

issues), but this will increase as the project nears the mid-stage and then decrease at the end of the project (so that consensus can be achieved).

- *Relationship conflict*—This type of conflict is never helpful. It usually will disguise itself as another type of conflict (task or process) and thus will often not be dealt with until it is too late.

1.00–2.00   Lunch

2.00–3.00   Conflict and Trust in Projects

Exercise

An exercise was designed to demonstrate the interplay between constructive conflict and the different types of conflict. Although the exercise appeared to be fairly easy, many individuals had difficulty in identifying the different types of conflict (most were able to identify the constructive and destructive graphs). This also provided an opportunity for individuals to chart and discuss their own conflict situation.

Conflict Styles and Strategy

Different people deal with conflict in a variety of ways and the best way to illustrate this was to introduce and use the Thomas Kilmann Conflict Mode Instrument (TKI). The participants were asked to complete the TKI earlier and the results were used as part of the discussion. (When an individual has completed the TKI, they receive a score, which identifies their conflict style preference and some of the characteristics of their style. The score also provided some guidance on when to use a particular style and signs of underuse and overuse.) This challenged participants to think of working with conflict in a different way—perhaps moving away from their preferred style of functioning to a situation that requires a specific strategy.

The TKI identified different styles (preferences) of dealing with conflict. The five styles are:
- Compete
- Avoid
- Compromise
- Accommodate
- Collaborate

The components of each style were explained to the group and were introduced on X–Y axis (cooperativeness = individual attempts to satisfy concerns of others; and assertiveness = individual attempts to satisfy own concerns).

Conflict Management Indicator

This is a short questionnaire that uses a conflict experience from the past to answer questions.

Exercise/Activity
- Completion of the short questionnaire
- Returned the questionnaire to the trainer
- Brief discussion of some of the issues this might have raised

Learning Objective
- Identified that conflict had a major negative impact in and outside of the workplace
- Examined the impact of conflict and how it has become a major factor in the workplace
- Established the importance of an effective conflict management process

This questionnaire gave individuals another way of thinking about a previous conflict and how it was managed. Several of the questions were quite probing (there was a question that asked about the destructiveness of the conflict). Because the questionnaires were collected, the trainers could compare the answers of a couple of different questions (this was useful particularly to a team leader who could then be able to understand how the team members had dealt with prior conflicts).

3.00–3.15   Break

3.15–4.30   Handling Difficult Conversations

Managing Relationships – Difficult Conversations
The session began by asking (and discussing) what made a conversation difficult. The trainers then introduced the concept that in general there are three different types of conversations:
- What happened—the back story
- Identity—what does this say about the person
- Feelings—what should people do with their emotions

Then the idea was introduced that individuals should think about three things (components) before engaging in a difficult conversation. The three components are:
- Preparation
- Emotion
- Feedback

Preparation
One of the most important and most overlooked elements is adequate preparation. When an individual is prepared to have a conversation,

they will have the confidence to engage appropriately; this is particularly essential when dealing with situations where facts/details are in question. The underlying theme is being prepared to know when and how to engage in a difficult conversation.

Emotions
When dealing with emotions there are three things that should be considered:
• Recognize the emotion (and emotional content of the conversation)
• Respect their emotion (and emotional reaction)
• Respond—deal with their emotion as well as your own

Also, when thinking about the conversation, it is helpful for individuals to move from:
• Certainty to curiosity
• Intention to impact
• Blame to contribution

Feedback
• Giving and receiving of feedback
• A necessary part of any managerial function
• Think of how feedback will be received by the other person
• Understand emotional reaction to feedback (by both giver and receiver)

Exercise/Activity
• Show an example of a difficult conversation that went well.
• Show an example of a difficult conversation that was unsuccessful.
• Think of a difficult conversation that you need to have.
• Complete the preparation sheet (to help understand how to prepare).
• Practice having a difficult conversation (in groups of three – taking turns, with each person having the conversation with another person while the third person was observing).

4.30–5.15 Viewing Group Video: Discussion of Personal Behaviors, Strengths, and Competences

Conflict Styles and Strategy Review
During this session, the trainer wrapped-up some of the information about conflict styles and strategy that will have been introduced throughout the day.
• The "'rope" exercise was replayed to the group.
• Divided into groups of four, each group was asked to watch the replay and observe the following:
  • Group 1 – Signs of different types of conflict
  • Group 2 – Signs of different conflict styles

- Group 3 – Comment on how the group interacted
- Group 4 – Comment on what learning points from the day were displayed

- Each group was asked to report back; then the discussion was opened up to the group for comments and draw out learning points. In particular there was a focus on (1) how the group interacted over the period of the exercise, (2) evolution of emotions and conflict in "project" time span, (3) identifying task, process, and relationship conflict, (4) identifying what (if any) styles of conflict were displayed, and (5) identifying how people were using emotional intelligence.

5.15–5.30   Summary of Day & Debrief

A brief review of the objectives from the beginning of the day. Discussed how they were covered and what (if any) additional comments the trainer/participants might have had.

5.30   Close

APPENDIX 1

Semi-Structured
Interview Schedule

Emotional Intelligence and Projects

1. Tell me about your recollections of the training program and what you think you gained most from your attendance.

(2) Can you give me any specific examples, since attending the training, where you have been in a situation and suddenly experienced or remembered something that reminded you of anything you covered on the EI training program?

(3) Can you tell me about a particular emotional event that took place recently that was covered in the training program?

(4) Can you tell me about a specific conflict situation that you have been involved in at work recently, how you approached it, and what the outcome was?

(5) Can you give me any examples over the past 6 months where the quality of the relationship between you and other colleagues on a project made a difference in the manner in which a problem was solved or addressed?

(6) Can you give me one or two major examples of how your feelings influenced a particular decision you made or a course of action you took during a project?

(7) Are there any specific examples you can provide where you consciously tried to imagine yourself in a colleague's shoes at work and how he or she might be thinking or feeling in response to a particular situation? What, if anything, happened and how do you think it affected what you did next?

(8) Is there anything you can think of where you attempted to change the way you thought, acted, or behaved as a result of the training program;

and which you think you have improved over the past 6 months through practice?

(9) In what ways if any, do you think you have considered how your feelings affect the way you act in projects or teams?

APPENDIX 2

Emotional Intelligence Training

EXERCISE 1—Emotional Self-Awareness: Confessors and Listeners (Based on Lynn, 2002)

The aim of this exercise is to improve your awareness and control of your own emotional responses, and the extent to which you produce emotional responses in others.

You need to pair off with a partner. In the first round, one of you will play the confessor while the other plays the listener. After the first round you will be asked to reflect on the content of the interaction.

Confessor

Think of a real personal weakness that you possess, for example, being prone to behaviors such as being short-tempered, domineering, too yielding, late, unreliable, disorganized, blaming others, obstructive, not eating properly, smoking, drinking, not taking exercise, sulking, etc.

The weakness should be real and significant enough to have some emotional feelings attached to it for you, but not so serious as would open a can of worms and give rise to the need for several sessions of psychotherapy.

You should then explain your weakness to your partner, like an admission and a bit of an explanation or guess as to the cause, for example: "I can be obstructive at times when I could be more helpful—perhaps it's when I'm feeling low and that people don't show me any respect," or "I come in late sometimes because I think 'why should I bother about doing a good job when I should be paid more.'"

After the short interaction, you will need to reflect and comment on it.

Listener

Firstly you are a listener, but more than that you are a CRITIC. You are about to listen to the confessor talking about a personal weakness. Your role is to demonstrate giving the confessor a **negative critical reaction** to their admission (don't go mad—we don't want any tears, please). Just a few sentences of blame, judgment, and an uncaring reaction (imagine the worst teacher you had at school and how they used to treat kids who messed up or misbehaved, or imagine a bullying boss you've known).

After the short interaction, you will need to reflect and comment on it.

TUTOR'S NOTES

Emotional Self-Awareness: Confessors and Listeners

The aim of this exercise is to improve your awareness and control of your own emotional responses, and the extent to which you produce emotional responses in others. You need to organize yourself with a partner into a pair. In the first round, one of you will play the confessor while the other plays the listener. After each round, you will be asked to reflect on the content of the interaction.

1. Ask pairs to decide who will be the confessor and listener for the first round.
2. Give out exercise sheets. Allow a few minutes for people to read through the instructions sheet and the additional personal reflections sheet.
3. Then start the role play for 5 minutes per round.
4. After 5 minutes of the first round of role play, ask the participants to stop and, without discussing with their partners, complete their personal reflections sheet. Ask participants to pause and think for a moment and try to consider how they are feeling as a result of what has just happened in the role play. Ask individuals to try to record their actual feelings.
5. Now ask participants to swap roles. After the second role play and an additional 5 minutes, ask them to stop and complete the self-reflection questionnaire again.
6. Come back to the large group and discuss in a plenary session.

Debrief

1. Emphasize that negative emotional responses to all sorts of situations, behaviors, and circumstances in work (and personal) contexts are always being generated and that they can often influence how we respond to people or the decisions we make, as well as our general moods.
2. Ask the participants about their emotional responses in the first round. Get their emotional responses on a flip chart.
3. Ask participants if they are aware of why they felt the way they did. How useful were these emotional responses? Record these on a flip chart and discuss in the large group.
4. Ask participants if they saw any signs of how their part was feeling, through their body language or other means of nonverbal communication. List these

on flip chart. Discuss in the large group how we can often reveal how we are feeling (and our thoughts and attitudes) unconsciously through the facial and bodily signals we communicate.

NEXT: Understanding Emotions

Tutor: I want us to think about how our emotional responses are sometimes connected to the events that trigger them. This is important because it can help us in thinking about how better to manage our own emotions and other people's.

5. Firstly, spend a few minutes thinking about a specific situation in which you regretted acting the way that you did in a work context. Spend a few minutes thinking about what you were feeling at the time and how you reacted. Think about how your emotions and behaviors were connected.

Tutor: Now give a brief presentation input on how irrational beliefs shape our emotional responses. This is important for understanding how emotions can develop.

6. Ask participants to write down whether there were any irrational beliefs going on. Ask whether individuals would be prepared to share some of the responses. Next ask participants whether they can identify what their beliefs were that may have caused their reactions. Try to identify both rational and irrational beliefs.

   Rational beliefs are those which are healthy, productive, and consistent with social reality. They generally consist of preferences, desires, and wants.

   Irrational beliefs are rigid, dogmatic, unhealthy, maladaptive, and mostly get in the way of our efforts to achieve our goals. IBs are comprised of demands, musts, and shoulds.

   The goal is to uncover hidden demands (shoulds), awfulizing, global, self-downing, and low frustration tolerance.

Emotional Self-Awareness Reflections

1. What were your feelings during the role play?

2. Why do you think you felt that way?

3. Were you aware of how your body was responding while you were feeling in the way you stated above? What was your partner was feeling?

APPENDIX 3

Emotional Intelligence Training

EXERCISE 2: PERCEIVING EMOTIONS

We are going to look at the video clip taken from the film *Erin Brockovich* starring Julia Roberts. The object of this exercise is for you to identify how emotion is communicated through a range of facial signals and other forms of nonverbal communication. Recognizing and understanding this emotional display plays a major part in effective communication, building rapport, and being able to influence ethically. Recognizing the emotional states of others can help us in making decisions about what to do next about particular problems or how to act in these circumstances.

Working in teams and projects generate significant emotions; knowing how these can originate in response to specific team behaviors and responding to them in others is a key skill.

In the scene that follows you will observe four people sitting around a large table Erin (Julia Roberts) is sitting next to Ed (Albert Finney), and they are sitting on the opposite side of the table from Theresa and Kurt. Try to make as many observations as you can regarding the nature of the interpersonal interactions occurring. Make as many notes as you can providing as much detail as you can of what you saw and heard.

Pay attention to the nonverbal communication including kinesthetics (body motion such as gestures, posture, and eye movement); paralanguage (voice quality such as tone, tempo, rhythm, and pitch) and proxemics (the use of personal space). Areas to look out for include:

1. How emotion(s) are communicated nonverbally through facial display and other forms of body language
2. The use of any illustrators such as gesturing with the hands or arms connected with any emotion(s)
3. Signs of any emotional display that you pick up through language including speech rate, volume, tempo and tone, as well as content.

4. The circumstances/situational context that precedes any emotion(s) you perceive

Perceiving Emotions Exercise

Consider the following questions:

1. What aspects of body language conveyed attempts at dominance?
2. What aspects of body language conveyed confidence or status?
3. How was the anxiety conveyed?
4. What aspects conveyed closer interpersonal ties?
5. What aspects of body language did you think either contributed to or impeded rapport between the individuals?
6. How was the emotion of anger conveyed (such as facial display and other forms of nonverbal communication).
7. Were there attempts at concealing emotion? If so, was there any leakage of the true emotion felt?
8. Do you think being more emotionally intelligent might have led to a different outcome here? If so, how?

TUTOR'S NOTES

Firstly, explain the objectives of the exercise.

In the scene that follows, you will observe four people sitting around a large table (Erin (Julia Roberts) is sitting next to Ed (Albert Finney), and they are sitting on the opposite side of the table from Theresa and Kurt. You will be able to watch the clip twice. Try to make as many observations as you can regarding the nature of the interpersonal interactions occurring. Make as many notes as you can, providing as much detail as you can from what you saw and heard and between whom. Pay particular attention to the areas identified on your handout.

After participants have watched the clip, replay the clip again, only this time with the sound down, so you can concentrate far more on the body language. Again make additional notes or comments as you wish.

Once participants have observed the scene twice, ask them to break into their groups and discuss the questions on Part 2.

Timings:	Watching clip:	5 minutes
	Working in groups:	15 minutes
	Watching clip	5 minutes
	Working in groups:	15 minutes
	Plenary and discussion:	20 minutes
	Total:	1 hour

APPENDIX 4

Emotional Intelligence Training

EXERCISE 3: VERBALLY DEMONSTRATING EMPATHY (Based upon Egan, 1976)

Empathy requires that you are able to communicate an understanding of an individual's feelings and the experiences and/or behaviors that underlie them.

These are the kinds of statements you might hear in the course of project working. Picture yourself listening to the speaker. This exercise should give you some experience of responding directly to the feelings of another.

Directions

(1) Read the statement, pause for a moment, and then write down the description of the speaker's feelings that comes to mind immediately. Note that in some cases, the speaker may be indicating more than one feeling for you to identify. Then focus on the content, which is the distinct behaviors or experiences that have given rise to these feelings. Try to imagine that the person is speaking directly to you

First you will use the somewhat artificial formula:

"You feel (word or words that indicate feelings) because (words indicating the content, experiences, and/or behaviors underlying feelings)."

For example:

Jeff

"I had a hard time coming back here today. I felt that I shared myself pretty extensively last week, even to the point of letting myself get angry. This morning I was wondering what kind of excuse I could make up for not being here."

a. You're feeling awkward about being in the group today because, given last week, you aren't sure how I or others, will receive you.

(2) Then reread the statements and check yourself for accuracy. The second time, see if you can come up with a better response to each statement by using your own language, making it as natural as possible, rather than using the formula.

    b.   Jeff, I know it's not easy being here today. You've been asking yourself how you're going to be received. In fact you're so uneasy that you almost didn't come.

1. Bill

"I wish I knew how best to respond to all of this. I know I messed up in getting the figures we needed in order to hit that deadline. I do value the honesty and feedback from the team. But it just makes me look at myself—my fears of failing and I know that the way I respond, when I try to talk over you, it is because I just get so defensive. I just wish I could deal with this more effectively."

    a...

    b...

2. Jess

"What do you mean we are not hitting the standards required in the specification? We are working flat out here and quite frankly I don't appreciate your interfering in my area of responsibility. I'm having to pull out all the stops for this one because you messed up on the original timescales that were given to the client. If anything, the problems we're having are because of you. I'm just not putting up with this anymore—its really getting me down."

    a...

    b...

3. Gary

"I really don't know how to deal with this anymore! You look so sincere, and I believe that you are sincere. I think that you actually have the project's interests at heart. You talk to me here and pull me up on my performance and contribution. But the way you do it! You keep after me. You make the same point over and over again. Sometimes I just want to run out of here screaming!"

    a...

    b...

4. Marie

"No, I haven't got the time to keep coming back to you on all of this. I'm fed up! The contract isn't so grey about who is responsible for the ongoing maintenance and repair of that particular track, as you keep saying. You say that four different people could read it and get a completely different interpretation. Well, this is going to cause major financial problems and put future contracts in jeopardy unless you sort this out now!"

a...

b...

EXERCISE 4: PRACTICING DEMONSTRATING EMPATHY (Based upon Egan, 1976)

The purpose of this exercise is to make you think about some dimensions of your interpersonal style and behavior, while at the same time, offer an opportunity for a partner to show some empathetic understanding of the issue you have just identified.

Directions

1. Choose some situation or issue or relationship having to do with your interpersonal style that you would like to take a deeper look into when working in teams or projects. Choose something that you can share with your partner without being overly uncomfortable.
2. You will spend about 8 minutes briefly describing the issue to your partner.
3. During that time your partner should attempt to convey an empathetic understanding of the issue you have raised.
4. At the end of the 8 minutes reverse roles.
5. Offer each other feedback on each other's strengths and weaknesses, giving constructive feedback to one another on how differing aspects of rapport or empathy were communicated.

TUTOR'S NOTES

I would now like us to think about the previous session a little and consider how individuals chose to communicate an empathetic response to their partners.

1. Firstly, can we hear from those who role-played the listener for the second time around and let me ask you how you decided to communicate empathy. Did any of you think beforehand how you would do this? If so, what did you decide to do during the interaction? Write these down. Individuals can write down what they think, if there was anything that the listener did that communicated empathy. Participants should call these out. Write up on flipchart.

2. What do we mean by empathy? Can we have some definitions? Then give the actual definition to participants. Write these up on other flipchart. What do we mean by rapport? Highlight how empathy is different from rapport but that empathy can lead to rapport. Identify from the list which is empathy and which is rapport.

    Demonstrating empathy in interpersonal relationships involves both recognizing and communicating the feelings of a colleague in a particular situation as well as an understanding of the behaviors or experiences that underlie these feelings.

    It has two major components, a cognitive component and an affective component.

    *   The cognitive component is associated with sensory acuity and requires some judgmental accuracy in recognizing the feelings being displayed.
    *   The affective component is the emotional response of the self to or with the other person's feelings (affect). This component requires that we are able to generate some felt sense of the emotion in order that we can identify with the feelings and thereby the individual involved.

3. Discuss some of the techniques for enhancing rapport.
4. DEBRIEF

    Ask participants to come back to the large group.

    a. How did participants feel the exercise went? How easy/difficult was it for people?
    b. How did people feel about discussing an aspect of their interpersonal style?
    c. Did anyone find the content to be useful in terms of handling or addressing the specific area they covered?
    d. Were individuals able to detect emotional cues? What were they?

APPENDIX 5

Emotional Intelligence Training

EXERCISE 5: ROLE PLAYS TO SHOW PRACTICE IN RAPPORT, EMPATHY, AND ANTICIPATING AND RESPONDING TO EMOTIONS

Role Play One: The Trophy Project (Based on Kerzner, 1998)

Background

Richard was involved with the Trophy project from its conception and was appointed as project manager when the company accepted the project to develop a new prototype. The program schedules started to slip from day one, and expenditures were excessive. Richard found that the functional managers were charging direct labor time to his project but working on their own pet projects. When Richard complained of this, he was told not to meddle in the functional manager's allocation of resources and budgeted expenditures. After approximately 6 months, Richard was requested to make a progress report directly to corporate headquarters.

Richard took this opportunity to bare his soul. The report substantiated that the project was forecasted to be 1 year behind schedule. Richard's staff, as supplied by line managers, was inadequate to maintain the required pace, let alone make up any time that had already been lost. The estimated cost at completion at this interval showed a cost overrun of at least 20%. This was Richard's first opportunity to tell his story to people who were in a position to correct the situation. The result of Richard's frank, candid evaluation of the Trophy project was predictable. Nonbelievers finally saw the light, and the line managers realized that they had a role to play in the completion of the project. Most of the problems were now out in the open and could be corrected by providing adequate staffing and resources. Corporate Headquarters ordered immediate remedial action and staff support to provide Richard a chance to bail out his program.

The results however were not at all what Richard had expected. He no longer reported to the project office; he now reported directly to the operations director. Corporate Headquarter's interest in the project became very intense, requiring a 7:00 a.m. meeting every Monday morning for complete review of the project status and plans for recovery. Richard soon found himself spending more time preparing paperwork, reports, and projections for his Monday morning meetings than he did administering the Trophy project. The main concern of the corporate head office was to get the project back on schedule. Richard spent many hours preparing the recovery plan and establishing staffing requirements to bring the project back onto its original schedule.

Corporate Headquarters, in order to closely track the progress of the Trophy project, assigned an assistant program manager. The assistant program manager determined that a sure cure for the Trophy project would be to computerize the various problems and track the progress through a very complex computer program. Corporate provided Richard with 12 additional staff members to work on the computer program. In the meantime, nothing changed. The functional managers still did not provide adequate staff for recovery, assuming that the additional manpower Richard had received from corporate would accomplish that task.

After approximately £50,000 was spent on the computer program to track the problems, it was found that the project objectives could not be handled by the system. Richard discussed the problems with a computer supplier and found that £15,000 more was required for programming and additional storage capacity. It would take 2 months for installation of the additional storage capacity and the completion of the programming. At this point, the decision was made to abandon the computer program.

Richard was now 1½ years into the project with no prototype units completed. The project was still 9 months behind schedule with the overrun projected at 40% of budget. Another problem that Richard had to contend with was that the vendors who were supplying components for the project were also running behind schedule. Richard had been providing reports to the customer on a regular basis and they were aware that the project was behind schedule. However, after receiving this latest update in a report from Richard, the customer telephoned and demanded a meeting to find out from Richard how this was all going to be sorted out.

Richard

Yesterday while in the office putting together a report for the client, a corporate vice president came into your office. "Richard", he said to you, "In any project I look at the top of the sheet of paper and the person whose name appears at the top of the sheet is the one I hold responsible. For this project, your name appears at the top of the sheet. If you cannot bail this thing out, you are in serious trouble in this corporation. You know you are being held responsible for the project and action needs to be taken."

First

Consider what you think your priorities are in order to (*a*) get the project back on track and (*b*) placate the customer.

Then

You are about to go into the meeting to explain to the customer how you intend to get the project back on track and a plan for recovery. Consider how you intend to use your emotional intelligence and interpersonal skills in order to respond to the customer effectively and try to secure the outcome from the meeting that you want.

Customer

You have been receiving reports from Richard on a timely basis and have been aware of the fact that the Trophy project was behind schedule. However, these delays and problems seem to be getting worse and you are now becoming extremely impatient with the seeming failure of Richard to steer the project satisfactorily. You now have major concerns that the Trophy project is in serious trouble.

You have decided that enough is enough and that a meeting between yourself and Richard is necessary in order to get to the bottom of this and for you to gain some assurance that the project will succeed.

You have decided that you want a number of outcomes from this meeting given that that project is currently running 6 to 8 months behind schedule. The first is some specifics from Richard as to how he intends to get the project back on track. The second is that you now require progress reports on a weekly rather than monthly basis in order to keep a tighter grip on what is going on. The third is that you wish to make arrangements to assign a representative in Richard's department to be "on-site" at the project on a daily basis and to interface with Richard and his staff as required. In this way you believe you could exercise greater control and make changes to the program as necessary.

Although you intend to be polite you are in no mood to be fobbed off!

Role Play Two: The Lyle Project (Based on Kerzner)

Atlay Co.:	Engineering Company
Vice-president of sales:	Greta Munz
Vice-president of procurement:	John Mabby
Project manager supervisor:	Sanjay Sesh
Preliminary project manager:	George Fitz (now relocated)
Project manager:	Chrissie Jung
Project purchasing agent:	Jennifer Shields

Lyle Co.:	Industrial Plastics Manufacturer
Vice-president of operations:	Fred Wilson

Background

In November Atlay's vice-president of sales (Greta Munz), was notified by Lyle's vice-president of operations (Fred Wilson) that Atlay had been awarded the US $600 million contract to design, engineer, and construct a polypropylene plant in Louisiana, USA.

Sanjay Sesh, the supervisor of project managers at Atlay, had initially appointed George Fitz, who had been responsible for handling the initial proposal, as project manager; however, 1 week later, George received a promotion and was relocated to another part of the company. Following this, Sanjay appointed Chrissie Jung to be project manager. Chrissie had been with the company for 15 years, starting as a project engineer, and had previously worked on two other smaller projects by comparison.

Approximately 1 week after being awarded the contract, Fred Wilson and his contingent from Lyle arrived at Atlay headquarters to go over details in the project specification. During this initial meeting, Fred emphasized that it was essential for the plant to be completed on time since their competitor was also in the process of preparing to build a similar facility in the same general location. The first plant that was finished would most likely be the one that would establish control over the southwestern U.S. market for polypropylene material. Mr Wilson felt that Lyle had a 6-week headstart over its competitor at the moment and wanted to increase that difference, if at all possible.

Next, the design package was handed over so that the process engineering stage of the project could begin. This package was, according to their inquiry letter, so complete that all material requirements for this job could be placed within 3 months after project award (since very little design work was required by Atlay on this project). Two weeks later, Chrissie contacted the lead process engineer on the project who informed her that the design package needed further development that would take about 6 weeks to straighten out, which meant adding a 6-week schedule delay to the 3 months' lead time to obtain materials.

The Atlay team, operating within a matrix organizational structure, plunged right into the project and was made aware of the delay. Chrissie instructed the team, however, to cut corners, whenever doing so might result in time savings. She also told team members to suggest to members of their functional departments who were working on this project, methods that could possibly result in quicker turnaround of the work required of them. Following Chrissie's instructions, the project team coerced the various engineering departments into operating outside of their normal procedures due to the special circumstances surrounding this job.

For example, the civil engineering section prepared a special preliminary structural steel package, and the piping engineering section prepared preliminary piping packages so that the purchasing department could go out to inquiry immediately. Normally, the purchasing department would have to wait for formal take-offs from both of these departments before they would send out inquiries to potential vendors. Operating in this manner could result in some problems, however. For example, the purchasing department might arrange for discounts from the vendors based on the quantity of structural steel estimated during the preliminary take-off. After the formal take-off has been done by the civil engineering department (about 1 month) they might find out that they underestimated the quantity of structural steel required on the project by about 50 tons. This would be damaging because knowing that this extra steel was required could have enabled the purchasing department to secure additional discounts.

To add to Chrissie's problems, she has just been informed that a 6,000-staff-hour overrun is forecast on the purchasing side of the project compared to that which had been estimated in the initial proposal by George Fitz, who put the proposal together. To deal with this, she decided to pass some of the purchasing directly to the subcontractors at the job site.

At the present time

It is now 2 weeks since Chrissie was selected to head up the project. She just returned to her desk and saw a message stating that John Mabby (vice-president of procurement) had called. She returns his call to discover that John Mabby wants a meeting with her tomorrow morning to discuss a number of concerns he has been hearing about the project. It seems as though he had had a rather lengthy discussion with Jennifer Shields, the project purchasing agent assigned to the Lyle project. During the course of that conversation, it became very apparent that this particular project is not operating within the normal procedures established for the purchasing department.

John Mabby

You are extremely angry and upset to have learned from Jennifer Shields that Chrissie has been operating outside normal operating procedures. You are acutely embarrassed that you never knew what was going on and believe that Chrissie made you look a fool in front of Jennifer (who reports to you) by keeping you in the dark.

You also firmly believe that Chrissie should have discussed any deviations with you in your role as Atlay's vice president of procurement, prior to instructing Jennifer, the purchasing agent on the project, to proceed in this manner.

Importantly, you would never have agreed to allow purchasing to work around the procedures and, in any event, you would have expected that Chrissie would have come to you first to discuss these changes to procedures.

You intend to tell Chrissie that as of this moment you have instructed the purchasing side on the project (Jennifer) that from now she is to check with you prior to going against any standard operating procedures. After all, Jennifer works in your department. You are the one who reviews her annual performance, approves the size of any raise, and/or determines whether she gets a promotion. Jennifer receives her directions from you.

In addition, you are not pleased that you have also been informed that there is going to be an additional 6,000-hour overrun on the purchasing side of the project and that Chrissie has not submitted an additional change request to the client.

You have now arranged to meet with Chrissie to let her know your views on these matters.

Chrissie Jung

Although you have handled two projects previously, those were much smaller than the Lyle project and you feel that you need to show that you can head up projects of this scale. You also know that it's very important that this job be completed in accordance with the Lyle requirements since they would be building two more similar plants within the next 10 years. A good effort on this job could further enhance Atlay's chances for being awarded the next two jobs.

The telephone call from John Mabby has left you feeling a little uneasy, but you are sure that you can explain that the design problems you encountered early on in the project viewed against the need to complete the project on time justified the actions you took and the requests that you made of the project team. After all, you are responsible for the project's success and satisfying the customer's requirements; and a lot is at stake. Furthermore, individuals assigned to you for this project should operate in accordance with your requests and expectations, whether they are within procedures or not.

You have also attempted to solve the predicted overrun on purchasing staff hours by passing some of the purchasing responsibilities directly to the subcontractor on site so you don't think those predicted hours will actually be needed now. Given that it was George Fitz who was responsible for underestimating purchasing requirements in the first place, you can hardly be blamed for the forecast overrun.

First

Consider what you think your priorities and outcomes are before going into this meeting.

Then

You are about to go into the meeting. Consider how you intend to use your emotional intelligence and interpersonal skills in order to respond to effectively and try to secure the outcome(s) from the meeting that you want.

Reference: Kerzner, H. Project Management Case Studies.

Role Play Three: The International City of Culture Project
Role One
Background to the Case

The Creative & Visual Arts Council has been a keen player in a major project to develop a new arts complex in a key city in the south of England which is setting its sights on becoming an international city of culture by 2026. Initial plans were drawn up for a modern 300- to 350-seat performance space with flexibility for configuring it into a variety of differing formats as well as a 120-seat studio with retractable seating. The aim of the new arts complex is to offer a wide range of arts and cultural events ranging from music, dance, theatre, and comedy/cabaret.

Although the city has a good basis from which to start with its diverse population and vibrant arts communities, its infrastructure is weak and there is a pressing need to invest significantly in creating cultural facilities for the 21st century. The proposal for this new arts complex is seen as a central component of plans for creating a vibrant cultural quarter in the city and in securing the prestigious title of international city of culture. The project has been going for 18 months with four key partners driving it, consisting of the city council, the regional economic development agency, the Creative & Visual Arts Council, Regional Arts members, alongside representatives from local arts groups and city development agencies.

Key stakeholders have already committed to the vast majority of capital funding and a considerable portion of the revenue finding. A project manager from the city council is leading the capital project and work has been underway for 6 months. However, the project schedule started to slip from day one, and expenditures are becoming excessive with already a considerable overspend being predicted. Funds still need to be raised from commercial sponsors and some of the arts partners are becoming increasingly concerned that the potential sponsors will put off investing in the project if something is not done to get the project back on track. The Creative & Visual Arts Council representative on the project recently spoke to the project manager from the city council but was told not to meddle in how the council allocated resources and budgeted expenditures for carrying out the project. At the beginning of the week, strategic partners on the project received a report confirming many of their fears that the project was forecast to now be almost 1 year behind schedule and that the estimated cost of completion at this interval showed a cost overrun of at least 20%. Contained in the report were also recommendations by the project manager that in order to try to contain expenditure, the proposed studio attached to the Arts Complex must be reduced in size to approximately 50% of its original proposed capacity. Many of the arts partners feel that this would severely restrict the range and type of arts that could be offered and believe that the Arts Council simply does not appreciate the implications of such a measure. Furthermore, they believe that the problem lies with how the capital project is being managed. Having now seen the report, the Creative & Visual Arts Council representative telephoned to arrange a meeting with the project manager from the city council to voice his concerns.

Creative & Visual Arts Council Representative

You have been receiving reports from the project manager on a timely basis and have been aware of the fact that the project was behind schedule. However, these delays and problems seem to be getting worse and you are now becoming extremely impatient with the seeming failure of the council project manager to steer the project satisfactorily. You now have major concerns that the project is in serious trouble.

You have major concerns that:

1. The continuing project schedule overrun will mean that many of the local arts groups planning to move into and use the Arts complex will have major problems in finding a suitable location to perform or display their work if the arts complex is not completed on time, and this will severely affect their financial positions and viability.

2. The excessive costs will deter other prominent corporate sponsors from investing in the project and is therefore creating additional risks in the longer-term success of the project.
3. The project manager's recommendation that the studio space be significantly reduced to address the project overspend will significantly affect the overall success of the project in being able to showcase the range of arts and cultural events that were envisaged, again significantly affecting what you consider to be one of the chief success factors.
4. You believe that there are problems with how the project is being managed, and that if these were addressed, the project could get back on track.

You have decided that enough is enough and that a meeting with the project manager is necessary in order to get to the bottom of all this and for you to gain some assurance that the project will succeed. You are in no mood to be fobbed off as too much is at stake and you want to avoid any bad publicity that might reflect badly on the Arts Council if the project is not seen to have been managed effectively and efficiently. You are about to go into this meeting.

Firstly, spend about 5 minutes deciding and writing down what outcomes you would like from this meeting given that the project is now running 6-8 months behind schedule.

Then consider how you will attempt to show empathetic understanding and use emotional intelligence abilities in order to try to secure the outcomes you have identified.

You have 15 minutes to try to secure the outcomes you want from the meeting.

Role Play Three: The International City of Culture Project
Role Two
Background to the Case

The Creative & Visual Arts Council has been a keen player in a major project to develop a new arts complex in a key city in the south of England which is setting its sights on becoming an international city of culture by 2026. Initial plans were drawn up for a modern 300- to 350-seat performance space with flexibility for configuring it into a variety of differing formats as well as a 120-seat studio with retractable seating. The aim of the new arts complex is to offer a wide range of arts and cultural events ranging from music, dance, theater, and comedy/cabaret.

Although the city has a good basis from which to start with its diverse population and vibrant arts communities, its infrastructure is weak and there is a pressing need to invest significantly in creating cultural facilities for the 21st century. The proposal for this new arts complex is seen as a central component of plans for creating a vibrant cultural quarter in the city and in securing the prestigious title of international city of culture. The project has been going for 18 months with four key partners driving it, consisting of the city administrative council, the regional economic development agency, the Creative & Visual Arts Council, and

Regional Arts delegates alongside representatives from local arts groups and city development agencies.

Key stakeholders have already committed to the vast majority of capital funding and a considerable portion of the revenue finding. A project manager from the city administrative council is leading the capital project and work has been underway for 6 months. However, the project schedule started to slip from day one, and expenditures are becoming excessive with already a considerable overspend being predicted. Funds still need to be raised from commercial sponsors and some of the arts partners are becoming increasingly concerned that the potential sponsors will be put off investing in the project if something is not done to get the project back on track. The Creative & Visual Arts Council representative on the project recently spoke to the project manager from the city administrative council but was told not to meddle in how the council allocated resources and budgeted expenditures for carrying out the project.

At the beginning of the week, strategic partners on the project received a report confirming many of their fears that the project was forecast to now be almost 1 year behind schedule and that the estimated cost of completion at this interval showed a cost overrun of at least 20%. Contained in the report were also recommendations by the project manager that in order to try to contain expenditure, the proposed studio attached to the arts complex must be reduced in size to approximately 50% of its original proposed capacity. Many of the arts partners feel that this would severely restrict the range and type of arts that would be offered and believe that the City Administrative Council simply does not appreciate the implications of such a measure. Furthermore, they believe that the problem lies with how the capital project is being managed. Having now seen the report, the Arts Council representative has decided to meet with the project manager from the city council to voice their concerns.

The City Council Capital Project Manager

You have been involved in the Arts Complex project since its inception and are the project manager responsible for the capital building component of the larger project. You have worked on a number of projects before but none as large as this one and it has proved challenging. A major problem is that the project is currently running about 6 to 8 months behind schedule and is heading for a 20% overspend.

There are a number of reasons why you think this has happened. Firstly, the total number of staff hours estimated for the project from the estates, planning, and finance departments in the council were too low at the outset and did not take into account the additional time that was needed to satisfactorily undertake the public consultation regarding the facilities on site at the proposed new Arts Center and how it can respond more effectively to local concerns over the potential environment impact of the Center. A local residents group raised a number of concerns regarding increased noise and traffic levels to the local area which held the project up in its early stages.

You also discovered that the heads of the departments for planning and estates have been charging direct labor time to your project but with staff actually working on their own pet projects. Your staff, as supplied by the head of department to work on the capital project, was inadequate to maintain the required pace, let alone make up any time that had already been lost due to the additional public consultation that was needed. You had a meeting with the chief executive of the City Council and these heads of departments a few weeks ago and they now seemed to realize that they had a role to play in the completion of the project. Most of the problems were now out in the open and could be corrected by providing adequate staffing and resources. Corporate headquarters ordered immediate remedial action and staff support to provide you with a chance to get the project on track.

However, although this should help to get the project back on schedule, the overspend remains a major problem and you put forward plans to reduce the planned studio build in order to try to get the project back within budget. You have recommended this in your last capital project update report to the other partners in the Arts Complex project but have not had any formal response yet. You received a telephone call from the Creative & Visual Arts Council representative yesterday asking to meet with you this morning to discuss the project. You expect there to be some strong views about your recommendation, but you believe the priority is to get the project back within budget and on schedule. However, you think that if you explain why the project fell behind schedule and how you are getting it back on track, it should be fine. You know the Creative & Visual Arts Council representative will probably focus on aesthetics and cultural aspects of the project but believe you can bring them round if you explain the importance of getting the project completed on time and within budget. You are about to go into this meeting.

Firstly, spend about 5 minutes deciding and writing down what outcomes you would like from this meeting.

Then consider how you will attempt to show empathetic understanding and use emotional intelligence abilities in order to try to secure the outcomes you have identified.

You have 15 minutes to try to secure the outcomes you want from the meeting.

OBSERVER SHEET

Your role is to observe the interaction that takes place between the two participants involved in the role play.

Specifically, you are looking for signs that either party is attempting to build rapport and demonstrate empathetic understanding, and for behaviors that might be thought to be either socio-emotional positive or socio-emotional negative. Look on the list below to familarize yourself with the behaviors that you need to watch out for. Note each time either person shows these behaviors by simply marking a tally (/) in each column under the appropriate person. Also note if either person shows any socio-emotive negative acts in a similar way. At the end of the session, you will need to provide feedback to both parties, so try to be as observant as you can. Feel free to make any written notes if you so wish.

At the end of the interaction, you need to complete the observer questionnaire attached to underpin your feedback to the interactants. Attached is also a criterion template for you to use to record your observations relating to specific communication, rapport, and empathy behaviors you observed between the two interactants.

OBSERVER SHEET FOR RECORDING OBSERVATIONS OF BEHAVIORS ASSOCIATED WITH EMPATHY, EMOTIONAL INTELLIGENCE, AND RAPPORT

You should use this as a basis for providing feedback to the interactants and for making your own judgments regarding the quality of the interaction on the Observer Feedback Sheet.

Rapport	Role Play Participant 1	Role Play Participant 2
Mirroring		
Attempts to pace/lead		
Forward lean		
Smiling at other person		
Adjusts proximity to other person		
Seeks eye contact		

Empathy		
Identifies with what other person is feeling		
Reflects back an understanding of feeling and why it is occurring		

Some Descriptors of What You Should Be Looking for During the Interaction:

Adaptors

Refer to manipulations of one's body such as rubbing, scratching, preening (often indicative of anxiety).

Eye Contact

The amount of time the interactants looked into each other's eyes.

Forward Lean

The time spent by the interactants maintaining a postural configuration in which their head was forward from the upright, vertical position relative to the hips.

Mutual Silence

Refers to the total time spent in which interactants were simultaneously silent for periods longer than 1.5 seconds.

Nervous Behavior

Any action or activity that suggests that someone is scared, anxious, uncomfortable or nervous (e.g., fidgeting, shaking, knees knocking, quivering voice, swallowing, and "freezing").

Proximity

The extent to which any individual attempts to shift the proximity between the interactants.

Synchrony

Refers to the extent to which the behaviors and the behavioral stream of each interactant were similar to and coordinated with (i.e. synchronized) each other. Manifestations of synchrony may take the form of mirroring, simultaneous movement, and coordinated movement.

Smiling

Refers to the total time spent by both interactants smiling.

OBSERVER FEEDBACK SHEET

1. **How would you rate the interaction that took place between the interactants on the following dimensions?**

1. Well-coordinated	Not at all	1	2	3	4	5	6	7	8	To a great extent
2. Boring	Not at all	1	2	3	4	5	6	7	8	To a great extent
3. Cooperative	Not at all	1	2	3	4	5	6	7	8	To a great extent
4. Harmonious	Not at all	1	2	3	4	5	6	7	8	To a great extent
5. Unsatisfying	Not at all	1	2	3	4	5	6	7	8	To a great extent
6. Uncomfortably paced	Not at all	1	2	3	4	5	6	7	8	To a great extent
7. Cold	Not at all	1	2	3	4	5	6	7	8	To a great extent
8. Awkward	Not at all	1	2	3	4	5	6	7	8	To a great extent
9. Engrossing	Not at all	1	2	3	4	5	6	7	8	To a great extent
10. Unfocused	Not at all	1	2	3	4	5	6	7	8	To a great extent
11. Involving	Not at all	1	2	3	4	5	6	7	8	To a great extent
12. Intense	Not at all	1	2	3	4	5	6	7	8	To a great extent
13. Unfriendly	Not at all	1	2	3	4	5	6	7	8	To a great extent
14. Active	Not at all	1	2	3	4	5	6	7	8	To a great extent
15. Dull	Not at all	1	2	3	4	5	6	7	8	To a great extent

2. Do you think that the interactants managed to communicate their perspectives of the situation to each other?
3. Do you think that either or both of the interactants successfully communicated their empathetic understanding of the other's perspectives?
4. To what extent did the Arts Council project manager attempt to build rapport? What if any impact did this have on the meeting outcome?

Any Additional Comments You Want to Make:

APPENDIX 6

Emotional Intelligence Training

EXERCISE 6: THE ORGANIZATION'S EMOTIONAL CLIMATE

Objectives:

1. To identify aspects of the organization's climate relating to emotional competence norms.
2. To identify how particular aspects of the organization's functioning and operations either help or impede the use of emotional competences.
3. To identify a list of key areas that could be targeted for change and action strategies for addressing them.

The emotional structure that a group adopts determines a group's level of emotional competence, which has been defined as the willingness to recognize, monitor, discriminate, and attend to emotion, and the ability to respond constructively to emotional challenge. As part of a collective emotional structure, emotionally competent norms are rules and expectations that influence group emotional competence and social capital.

Timing: **First set of questions:** (60 minutes)

              Voting: (5 minutes)

              Working on Action: (20 minutes)

Provide three examples of how conflict is typically viewed and dealt with in the organization. (10 + 5 minutes)

Provide three examples of how the organization typically recognizes and then deals with staff feelings. (10 + 5 minutes)

Provide three examples of how trust between the organization and its partners is typically perceived on projects. (10 +5 minutes)

Provide three examples of how the organization deals with uncertainty. (10 + 5 minutes)

The basic format of the activity is:

The whole gathering is asked a question. The teams confer among themselves and appointed spokespeople give the answers for their own team in turn. Guide the teams towards discussing and selecting the best three from within their own team. After an agreed/suitable time period, each team's spokesperson gives their team's answers in turn, which are recorded by the facilitator on stage or at the front of the auditorium, on a suitable viewing system (flip-chart sheets and blu-tack are perfectly okay if you like to use them) so all teams can see every other team's answers.

All the answers for a question are reviewed, and then voted on to identify which answer(s) are considered to be the best by all teams, or a 1-2-3 ranking of the three best-liked answers.

Review and invite questions and comments from the participants.

Then ask the teams to cast votes for each of the other team's answers, by which the facilitator then allocates scores for each team. The scoring system for the activity is flexible at the discretion of the facilitator, but must obviously be consistent and fair. For example, ask each team to confer and award three votes for the best answer, two points for second-best, and one point for third-best.

Example of next question:

Next, consider and suggest three ways that the organization can improve the key area that you have identified. (20 minutes)

References

Adair, J. (1979). *Action centred leadership.* London: Gower.

Amabile, T., Barsade, S., Mueller, J., & Staw, B. (2005). Affect and creativity at work. *Administrative Science Quarterly, 50,* 367–403.

Antonakis, J. (2003). Why emotional intelligence does not predict leadership effectiveness. *The International Journal of Organizational Analysis, 11,* 355–361.

Antonakis, J., Avolio, B., & Sivasubramaniam, H. (2003). Context and leadership: An examination of the nine-factor full range leadership theory using the multifactor leadership questionnaire. *Leadership Quarterly, 14*(3), 261–96.

Ashkanasy, N. N., & Tse, B. (2000). Transformational leadership as management of emotion: A conceptual review. In N. M. Ashkanasy, C. E. J. Hartel, & W. J. Zerbe (Eds.), *Emotions in the workplace: Research, theory and practice.* (pp. 221–235). Westport, CT: Quorum Books.

Atkins, P. W. B., & Wood, R. E. (2002). Self-versus others' ratings as predictors of assessment center ratings: Validation evidence for 360 degree feedback programs. *Personnel Psychology, 55,* 871–904.

Atwater, L. E., & Yammarino, F. J. (1992). Does self-other agreement on leadership perceptions moderate the validity of leadership and performance predictions? *Personnel Psychology, 45*, 141–164.

Atwater, L. E., & Yammarino, F. J. (1993). Personal attributes as predictors of superiors' and subordinates' perceptions of military academy leadership. *Human Relations, 46*, 645–668.

Ayoko, O. B., Callan, V. J., & Hartel, C. E. J. (2008). The influence of emotional intelligence climate on conflict and team members' reactions to conflict. *Small Group Research, 39*(2), 121–149.

Azjen, I. (1991). The theory of planned behavior. *Organizational Behavior and Human Decision Processes, 50*, 179–211.

Bagshaw, M. (2000). Emotional intelligence—Training people to be affective so they can be effective. *Industrial and Commercial Training, 32*(2), 61–65.

Baker, B. N., Murphy, D. C., & Fisher, D. (1983). Factors affecting project management success. In D. I. Cleland, & W. R. King (Eds.), *Project management handbook* (pp. 669–685). New York: Van Nostrand Reinhold.

Baldwin, T. T., & Ford, J. K. (1988). Transfer of training: A review and directions for future research. *Personnel Psychology, 41*, 63–105.

Bandura, A. (1986). *Social foundations of thought and action: A social-cognitive view.* Englewood Cliffs, NJ: Prentice Hall.

Barbuto, J. E., & Burbach, M. E. (2006). The emotional intelligence of transformational leaders: A field study of elected officials. *The Journal of Social Psychology, 146*(1), 51–64.

Barki, H., & Hartwick, J. (2004). Conceptualising the construct of interpersonal conflict. *International Journal of Conflict Management, 15*(3), 216–244.

Barling, J., Slater, F., & Kelloway, E. K. (2000). Transformational leadership and emotional intelligence: An exploratory study. *Leadership & Organization Development Journal, 21*(3), 157–161.

Bar-On, R. (1997). Bar-On Emotional Quotient Inventory: A measure of emotional intelligence, *Technical Manual.* Toronto: Multi-Health Systems.

Barsade, S. G. (2002). The ripple effect: emotional contagion and its influence on group behavior. *Administrative Science Quarterly, 47*, 644–675.

Bass, B. M. (1998). *Transformational Leadership.* Mahwah, NJ: Lawrence Erlbaum Associates,

Bass, B. M., & Avolio, B. J. (1994). *Improving organizational effectiveness through transformational leadership.* London: Sage.

Bass, B. M., & Avolio, B. J. (1997). Full range of leadership development manual for the Mulifactor Leadership Questionnaire. Palo Alto, CA: Mindgarden.

Bass, B. M., & Avolio, B. (2000). *MLQ mulitfactor leadership questionnaire* (2nd ed). Redwood City, CA: Mind Garden Inc.

Bass, B. M., Avolio, B. J., Jung, D., & Berson, Y. (2003). Predicting unit performance by assessing transformational and transactional leadership. *Journal of Applied Psychology, 88*, 207–218.

Beckett, D. (1999). Past the guru and up the garden path: The new organic management learning. In D. Boud & J. Garrick (Eds.), *Understanding Learning at Work* (pp. 3–97). London: Routledge.

Bishop, J. W., & Scott, K. D. (2000). An examination of organizational and team commitment in a self-directed team environment. *Journal of Applied Psychology, 85,* 439–50.

Bodtker, A. M., & Jameson, J. K. (2001). Emotion in conflict formation and its transformation: Application to organizational conflict management. *International Journal of Conflict Management, 12*(3), 259–275.

Bommer, W. H., Rubin, R. S., & Baldwin, T. T. (2004). Setting the stage for effective leadership: Antecedents of transformational leadership behavior. *The Leadership Quarterly, 15,* 195–210.

Bommer, W. H., Rich, G. A., & Rubin, R. S. (2005). Changing attitudes about change: Longitudinal effects of transformational leader behavior on employee cynicism about organizational change. *Journal of Organizational Behavior, 26*(7), 733–753.

Bono, J. E., & Judge, T. A. (2004). Personality and transformational and transactional leadership: A meta-analysis. *Journal of Applied Psychology, 89*(5), 901–910.

Boud, D., & Garrick, J. (2001). *Understanding learning at work.* London: Routledge.

Boyzatis, R. E., Goleman, D., & Rhee, K. S. (2000). Clustering competence in emotional intelligence: Insights from the Emotional Competence Inventory. In R. Bar-On & J. D. A. Parker (Eds.), *The handbook of emotional intelligence: Theory, development and assessment, and application at home, school and in the workplace.*, San Franciso, CA: Jossey-Bass.

Brackett, M. A., & Mayer, J. D. (2003). Convergent, discriminate and incremental validity of competing measures of emotional intelligence. *Personality and Social Psychology Bulletin, 29*(9), 1147–1158

Brackett, M. A., Mayer, J. D., & Warner, R. M. (2004). Emotional intelligence and the prediction of behavior. *Personality and Individual Differences, 36,* 1387–1402.

Brackett, M. A., Rivers, S. E., Shiffman, S., Lerner, N., & Salovey, P. (2006). Relating emotional abilities to social functioning: A comparison of self-report and performance measures of emotional intelligence. *Journal of Personality & Social Psychology, 91,* 780–795.

Brems, C., Baldwin, M., & Baxter, S. (1993). Empirical evaluation of a self psychologically oriented parent education program. *Family Relations: Interdisciplinary Journal of Applied Family Studies, 42,* 26–30.

Bresnen, M., & Marshall, N. (2000). Building partnerships: Case studies of client-contractor collaboration in the UK. *Construction Management Economics, 18,* 819–832.

Briner, W., Geddes, M., & Hastings, C. (1990). *Project Leadership.* Aldershot: Gower Publishing Company.

Brown, J. S., & Duguid, P. (1991). Organizational learning and communities of practice: Toward a unified view of working, learning and innovation. *Organization Science, 2*(1), 40–57.

Burgess, R., & Turner, S. (2000). Seven features for creating and sustaining commitment. *International Journal of Project Management, 18*(4), 225–233.

Butler, C. J., & Chinowsky, P. S. (2006). Emotional intelligence and leadership behaviour in construction executives. *Journal of Management in Engineering, 22*(3), 119–125.

Campbell, D. T., & Stanley, J. C. (1963). *Experimental and Quasi-Experimental Designs for Research.* Chicago: Rand McNally College Publishing.

Carless, S. A., Mann, L., & Wearing, A. J. (1998). Leadership, managerial performance and 360 degree feedback. *Applied Psychology: An International Review, 47,* 481–496.

Carmeli, A. (2003). The relationship between emotional intelligence and work attitudes, behavior and outcomes: An examination among senior managers. *Journal of Managerial Psychology, 18,* 788–813.

Caruso, D. R., Mayer, J. D., & Salovey, P. (2002). Relation of an ability measure of emotional intelligence to personality. *Journal of Personality Assessment, 79,* 306–320.

Caruso, D. R., & Wolfe, C. J. (2001). Emotional intelligence in the workplace. In J. Ciarrochi, J. P. Forgas, & J. D. Mayer (Eds.), *Emotional intelligence in everyday life* (pp. 150–167). New York: Psychology Press.

Chen, M-H. (2006). Understanding the benefits and detriments of conflict on team creativity process. *Creativity and Innovation, 15*(1), 105–116.

Cherniss, C., & Caplan, R. D. (2001). Implementing emotional intelligence programs in organizations. In C. Cherniss & D. Goleman (Eds.), *The emotionally intelligent workplace* (pp. 132–155). San Francisco: Jossey-Bass.

Cherniss, C., Goleman, D., Emmerling, R., Cowan, K., & Adler, M. (1998). Bring emotional intelligence to the workplace: A technical report issued by the consortium for research on emotional intelligence in organizations. Retrieved 27 March 2008 from *www.eiconsortium.org*

Ciarrochi, J. V., Chan, A. Y., & Caputi, P.(2000). A critical evaluation of the emotional intelligence concept. *Personality & Individual Differences, 28,* 539–561.

Cicmil, S., & Marshall, D. (2005). Insights into collaboration at the project level: Complexity, social interaction and procurement mechanisms. *Building Research & Information, 33*(6), 523–535.

Cicmil, S., & Hodgson, D. (2006). New possibilities for project management theory: A critical engagement, *Project Management Journal, 37*(3), 111–122.

Cicmil, S., Williams, T., Thomas, J., & Hodgson, D. (2006). Rethinking project management: Researching the actuality of projects. *International Journal of Project Management,* 675–686.

Clark, S. C., Callister, R., & Wallace, R. (2003). Undergraduate management skills courses and students' emotional intelligence. *Journal of Management Education, 27*(1), 3–23.

Clarke, N. (in press). Emotional intelligence abilities and their relationships with team processes. *Team Performance Management.*

Clarke, N. (2001). The impact of inservice training in social services. *British Journal of Social Work, 31*(5), 757–774.

Clarke, N. (2002). Job/work environment factors influencing training effectiveness within a human service agency: Some indicative support for Baldwin & Ford's transfer climate construct. *International Journal of Training and Development, 6*(3), 146–162.

Clarke, N. (2006a). Developing emotional intelligence through workplace learning: Findings from a case study in healthcare. *Human Resource Development International, 9*(4), 447–465.

Clarke, N. (2006b). Emotional intelligence training: A case of caveat emptor. *Human Resource Development Review, 5*(4), 1–20.

Clarke, N. (2006C). The limitations of in-service training in social services. In S. Sambrook & J. Stewart (Eds.), *Human resource development in the public sector: The case of health and social care* (pp. 315–340). London: Routledge.

Clarke, N. (2007a). Emotional Intelligence and Team Learning. Paper presented at the 4th Research in Work and Learning Conference, Cape Town, South Africa, December 2007.

Clarke, N. (2007b). Can we develop emotional intelligence in managers? *Proceedings of the Eighth University Forum for Human Resource Development Conference,* Oxford, UK, June 2007.

Cleland, I. C. (1995). Leadership and project management body of knowledge. *International Journal of Project Management, 13*(2), 83–88.

Cliffordson, C. (2002). The hierarchical structure of empathy: Dimensional organization and relations to social functioning. *Scandinavian Journal of Psychology, 43,* 49–59.

Coffey, A., & Atkinson, P. (1996). *Making sense of qualitative data: Complementary research strategies.* London: Sage.

Cohen, S. G., & Bailey, D. E. (1997). What makes teams work: Group effectiveness research from the shop floor to the executive suite. *Journal of Management, 23,* 239–290.

Colquitt, J. A., Lepine, J. A., & Noe, R. A. (2000). Toward an integrative theory of training motivation: A meta-analytic path analysis of 20 years of research, *Journal of Applied Psychology, 85*(5), 678–707.

Conlon, T. J. (2004). A review of informal learning literature, theory and implications for practice in developing global professional competence. *Journal of European Industrial Training, 28,* 283–295.

Conte, J. M. (2005). A review and critique of emotional intelligence measures. *Journal of Organizational Behavior, 26*(4), 433–440.

Cooke-Davies, T. (2002). The real success factors on projects. *International Journal of Project Management, 20*(3), 185–190.

Cooper, R. K., & Sawaf, A. (1997). *Executive EQ: Emotional intelligence in leadership and organizations.* New York: Grossett/Putnam.

Cowie, G. (2003). The importance of people skills for project managers. *Industrial and Commercial Training, 35*(6), 256–258.

Crawford, L. H. (2005). Senior management perceptions of project management competence. *International Journal of Project Management, 23*(1), 7–16.

Crawford, L. H., Hobbs, J. B., & Turner, J. R. (2005). *Project categorization systems: Aligning capability with strategy for better results.* Newtown Square, PA: Project Management Institute.

Crawford, L., Morris, P., Thomas, J., & Winter, M. (2006). Practitioner development: From trained technicians to reflective practitioners. *International Journal of Project Management, 24*, 722–733.

Creswell, J. W. (1998). *Qualitative inquiry and research design: Choosing among five traditions.* London: Sage.

Cromwell, S. E., & Kolb, J. A. (2004). An examination of work-environment support factors affecting training transfer of supervisory skills training to the workplace. *Human Resource Development Quarterly, 15*(4), 449–471.

Cunningham, M. R., & Elmhurst, C. (1977). Personality and the structure of the nonverbal communication of emotion. *Journal of Personality, 45*(4), 564–584.

Daus, C. S., & Ashkanasy, N. M. (2005). The case for the ability-based model of emotional intelligence in organizational behaviour. *Journal of Organizational Behavior, 226*, 453–466.

Davies, M., Stankov, L., & Roberts, R. D. (1998). Emotional intelligence: In search of an elusive construct. *Journal of Personality and Social Psychology, 75*(4), 989–1015.

Davis, M. H. (1983). Measuring individual differences in empathy: Evidence for a multidimensional approach. *Journal of Personality and Social Psychology, 44*, 113–126.

Dawda, D., & Hart, S. D. (2000). Assessing emotional intelligence: Reliability and validity of the Bar-On Emotional Quotient Inventory (EQ-i) in university students. *Personality and Individual Differences, 28*, 797–812.

Day, A. L., & Carroll, S. A. (2004). Using an ability-based measure of emotional intelligence to predict individual performance, group performance, and group citizenship behaviors. *Personality and Individual Differences, 36*, 1443–1458.

Decker, B., Landceta, R. E., & Kotnour, T. G. (2009). Exploring the relationships between emotional intelligence and the use of knowledge transfer methods in the project environment. *Knowledge Management Research and Practice, 7*(1), 15–36.

Denzin, N. K., & Lincoln, Y. S. (1994). *Handbook of qualitative research.* London: Sage.

Donnelian, M. B., Conger, R. D., & Burzette, R. G. (2007). Personality development from late adolescence to young adulthood: Differential stability, normative stability and evidence for the maturity-stability hypothesis. *Journal of Personality, 75*(2), 237–264.

Downey, L., Papageorgiou, V., & Stough, C. (2005). Examining the relationship between leadership, emotional intelligence and intuition in senior female managers. *Leadership & Organization Development 27*(4), 250–264.

Drouin, N., Bourgault, M., Bartholomew, Saunders, S. (2008). Investigation of contextual factors in shaping HR approaches and determining the success of international joint venture projects: Evidence from the Canadian Telecom Industry. *International Journal of Project Management, 27*(40), 344–354, available online 23 August 2008, from http://www.sciencedirect.com/science?_ob=ArticleURL&_udi=B6V9V-4T8R1VR.

Druskat, V., & Druskat, P. (2006). Applying emotional intelligence in project working. In S. Pryke & H. Smyth (Eds.), *The management of complex projects: A relationship approach* (pp. 78–96). Oxford: Blackwell.

Druskat, V. U., & Wolff, S. B. (2001). Building the emotional intelligence of groups. *Harvard Business Review, 79*(3), 81–90.

Druskat, V. U., & Wolff, S. B. (2001). Group emotional competence and its influence on group effectiveness. In C. Cherniss & D. Goleman (Eds.), *The emotionally intelligent workplace* (pp. 132–155). San Francisco: Jossey-Bass.

Duan, C., & Hill, C. E. (1996). The current state of empathy research. *Journal of Counseling Psychology, 43*, 261–274.

Dulewicz, V., & Higgs, M. J. (2003). Design of a new instrument to assess leadership dimensions and styles. *Henley Working Paper Series,* HWP 0311. Henley-on-Thames, UK: Henley Management College.

Dulewicz, V., & Higgs, M. (2004). Can emotional intelligence be developed? *International Journal of Human Resource Management, 15*(1), 95–111.

Dulewicz, V., Higgs, M., & Slaski, L. (2003). Measuring emotional intelligence: Content, construct and criterion validity. *Journal of Managerial Psychology, 18(5)*, 405–420.

Dvir, D., Raz, T., & Shenhar, A. J. (2003). An empirical analysis of the relationship between project planning and project success. *International Journal of Project Management, 21*(2), 89–95.

Dvir, D., Ben-David, A., Sadeh, A., & Shenhar, A. J. (2006). Critical managerial factors affecting defense project success: A comparison between neural network and regression analysis. *Engineering applications of artificial intelligence, 19*, 535–543.

Dyer, W. (1995). *Team building: Current issues and alternatives* (3rd ed). New York: Addison-Wesley.

Egan, G. (1976). *Interpersonal living: A skills/contract approach to human relations training in groups.* Florence, KY; Wadsworth Publishing (Cengage Learning).

Eisenbach, R., Watson, K., & Pillai, R. (1999). Transformational leadership in the context of organizational change. *Journal of Organizational Change Management, 12*(2), 80–89.

Eisenberg, N., & Miller, P. (1987). Empathy and prosocial behavior. *Psychological Bulletin, 101*, 91–119.

Elfenbein, H. (2006). Learning in emotion judgements: Training and the cross-cultural understanding of facial expressions. *Journal of Nonverbal Behavior, 30*, 21–36.

El-Sabaa, S. (2001). The skills and career path of an effective project manager, *International Journal of Project Management, 19*(1), 1–7.

Erdem, F., & Ozen, J. (2003). Cognitive and affective dimensions of trust in developing team performance. *Team Performance Management, 9*(5–6), 121–135.

Erera, P. I. (1997). Empathy training for helping professionals: Model and evaluation. *Journal of Social Work Education, 33*, 245–260.

Feyerherm, A. E., & Rice, C. L. (2002). Emotional intelligence and team performance: The good, the bad and the ugly. *The International Journal of Organizational Analysis, 10*(4), 343–362.

Fishbein, M., & Azjen, I. (1975). *Belief, attitude, intention and behavior: An introduction to the theory and research.* Reading, MA: Addison-Wesley.

Flanagan, J. C. (1954). The critical incident technique. *Psychgological Bulletin, 51*(4), 327–58.

Fleishman, E. A. (1974). Leadership climate, human relations training and supervisory behaviour. In E. A. Fleisham & A. R. Bass (Eds.), *Studies in Personnel and Industrial Psychology* (3rd ed.). Chicago, IL: Dorsey Press.

Ford, J. K., Kozlowski, S., Kraiger, K., Salas, E., & Teachout, M. (Eds.). (1997). Improving training effectiveness in work organizations. Mahwah, NJ: Erlbaum Associates Inc.

Ford, J. K., & Weissbein, D. A. (1997). Transfer of training: an updated review and analysis. *Performance Improvement Quarterly, 10*, 22–41.

Fox, S., & Spector, P. E. (2000). Relations of emotional intelligence, practical intelligence, general intelligence, and trait affectivity with interview outcomes: Its not all just "G". *Journal of Organizational Behavior, 21*, 203–220.

Frame, D. J. (1995). *Managing projects in organizations. How to make the best use of time, techniques and people.* San Francisco: Jossey-Bass.

Frayne, C., & Latham, G. P. (1987). Application of social learning theory to employee self management of attendance. *Journal of Applied Psychology, 72*, 387–392.

Friedman, H. S., & Riggio, R. E. (1981). Effect of individual differences in nonverbal expressiveness on transmission of emotion. *Journal of Nonverbal Behavior, 6*, 96–104.

Furnham, A. (1999). *Body language at work.* London: CIPD.

Gardner, H. (1983). *Multiple intelligences: The theory in practice.* New York: Basic Books.

Gardner, W. L., & Avolio, B. J. (1998). The charismatic relationship: A dramaturgical perspective. *Academy of Management Review, 23*, 32–58.

Gardner, L., & Stough, C. (2002). Examining the relationship between leadership and emotional intelligence in senior level managers. *Leadership and Organization Development Journal, 23*(2), 68–78.

George, J. M. (2000). Emotions and leadership: The role of emotional intelligence. *Human Relations, 53*, 1027–1055.

George, J. M., & Brief, A. P. (1992). Feeling good—doing good: A conceptual analysis of the mood at work-organizational spontaneity relationship. *Psychology Bulletin, 112*, 310–329.

George, J. M., & Jones, G. R. (2001). Towards a process model of individual change in organizations. *Human Relations, 54*, 419–444.

Gillford, R. (2006). Personality and nonverbal behaviour: A complex conumdrum. In V. Manusov & M. L. Patterson (Eds.), *The Sage handbook of nonverbal communication* (pp. 159–179). Thousand Oaks, CA: Sage.

Gist, M. E. (1987). Self efficacy: Implications for organizational behavior and human resource management. *Academy of Management Review, 12*, 472–485.

Gist, M. E., Schwoerer, C., & Rosen, B. (1989). Effects of alternative training methods on self efficacy and performance in computer software training. *Journal of Applied Psychology, 74*, 884–891.

Gist, M. E., Stevens, C. K., & Bavetta, A. G. (1991). Effects of self-efficacy and post-training intervention on the acquisition and maintenance of complex interpersonal skills. *Personnel Psychology, 44*, 837–861.

Gladstein, G. A. (1983). Understanding empathy: Integrating counseling, developmental, and social psychological perspectives. *Journal of Counseling Behavior, 34*, 467–482.

Goldberg, L. R., Johnson, J. A., Eber, H. W., Hogan, R., Ashton, M. C., Cloninger, C. R., & Gough, H. C. (2006). The international personality item pool and the future of public-domain personality measures. *Journal of Research in Personality, 40*, 84–96.

Goldberg, L. R. (1999). A broad-bandwidth, public domain, personality inventory measuring the lower-level facets of several five-factor models. In I. Mervielde, I. Deary, F. De Fruyt, & F. Ostendorf (Eds.), *Personality Psychology in Europe*, Vol 7, (pp. 7–28). Tilburg, The Netherlands: Tilburg University Press.

Goldenberg, I., Matheson, K., & Mantler, J. (2006). The assessment of emotional intelligence: A comparison of performance-based and self-report methodologies. *Journal of Personality Assessment, 86*(1), 33–45.

Goldstein, A. P., & Micheals, G. Y. (1985). *Empathy: Development, training and consequences.* Hillsdale, NJ: Lawrence Erlbaum.

Goldstein, I. L. (1993). Training in organizations: Needs assessment, development and evaluation (3rd ed). Monterey, CA: Brooks/Cole.

Goleman, D. (1995). *Emotional intelligence.* New York: Bantham.

Goleman, D. (1998). *Working with emotional intelligence.* New York: Bantham.

Goleman, D., Boyzatis, R. R., & McKee, A. (2002). Primal leadership. Boston: HBS Press.

Graen, G. B., & Uhl-Bien, M. (1995). Relationship-based approach to leadership: Development of leader-member exchange (LMX) theory of leadership over 25 years: Applying a multi-level multi-domain perspective. *Leadership Quarterly, 6*(2), 219–247.

Gross, R. D. (1987). *Psychology: The science of mind and behaviour.* Edward Arnold.

Groves, K. S. (2006). Leader emotional expressivity, visionary leadership, and organizational change. *Leadership and Organizational Development Journal, 27*(7), 566–583.

Groves, K. S., McEnrue, M. P., & Shen, W. (2008). Developing and measuring the emotional intelligence of leaders. *Journal of Management Development, 27*(2), 225–250.

Grundy, T. (2000). Strategic project management and strategic behavior. *International Journal of Project Management, 18*, April, 93–103.

Hall, A. J., & Bernieri, F. J. (Eds.). (2001). *Interpersonal sensitivity: Theory and measurement.* Mahwah, NJ: Erlbaum.

Hartman, F. (2000). *Don't park your brain outside.* Newton Square, PA: Project Management Institute.

Haynes, N. S., & Love, P. E. D. (2004). Psychological adjustment and coping among construction project managers. *Construction Management and Economics, 22,* 129–140.

Herbek, T. A., & Yammarino, F. J. (1990). Empathy training for hospital staff nurses. *Group and Organization Management, 15,* 279–295.

Herold, D. M., Fedor, D. B., Caldwell, J., & Liu, Y. (2008). The effects of transformational and change leadership on employees' commitment to a change: A multi-level study. *Journal of Applied Psychology, 93*(2), 346–357.

Higgs, M., & Rowland, D. (2002). Does it need emotional intelligence to lead change? *Journal of General Management, 27*(3), 62–76.

Hill, R. E. (1977). Managing interpersonal conflict in project teams. *Sloan Management Review, 18*(2), Winter, 45–61.

Hodgson, D., & Cicmil, S. (Eds.). (2006). *Making projects critical.* New York: Palgrave MacMillan Publishing.

Hogan, R., & Ones, D. S. (1997). Conscientiousness and integrity at work. In R. Hogan, J. A. Johnson, & D. R. Briggs (Eds.), *Handbook of Personality Psychology,* (pp. 849–870). San Diego, CA: Academic Press.

House, R. J., & Podsakoff, P. M. (1994). Leadership effectiveness: Past perspectives and future directions for research. In J. Greenberg (Ed.), *Organizational behavior: The state of the science* (pp. 45–82). Hillsdale, NJ: Lawrence Erlbaum Associates.

Humphrey, R. H. (2002). The many faces of emotional leadership. *The Leadership Quarterly, 13,* 493–504.

Huy, Q. N. (1999). Emotional capability, emotional intelligence and radical change. *Academy of Management Review, 24*(2), 325–345.

Huy, Q. N. (2002). Emotional balancing of organizational continuity and radical change: The contribution of middle managers. *Administrative Science Quarterly, 47,* 31–69.

Ibbertson, A., & Newell, S. (1998). Outdoor management development: The mediating effect of the client organisation. *International Journal of Training & Development, 2*(4), 239–258.

Ickes, W. (Ed.). (1997). *Empathic accuracy.* London: Guilford Press.

Ilarda, E., & Findlay, B. M. (2006). Emotional intelligence and propensity to be a teamplayer. *E-Journal of Applied Psychology: Emotional Intelligence. 2*(2), 19–29.

Isen, A. M., & Daubman, K. A. (1984). The influence of affect on categorization. *Journal of Personality and Social Psychology, 47,* 1206–1217.

Johnson, B., Lorenz, E., & Lundrall, B. A. (2002). Why all this fuss about codified and tacit knowledge? *Industrial and Corporate Change, 11*(2), 245–262.

Jones, G. R., & George, J. M. (1998). The experience and evolution of trust: Implications for cooperation and teamwork. *Academy of Management Review, 23*, 531–546.

Jordan, P. J., & Ashkanasy, N. M. (2006). Emotional intelligence, emotional self-awareness and team effectiveness. In V. U. Druskat, F. Sala, & G. Mount (Eds.), *Linking emotional intelligence and performance at work* (pp. 145–164). London: Lawrence Erlbaum Associates.

Jordan, P. J., Ashkanasy, N. M., Hartel, C. E. J., & Hooper, G. S. (2002). Workgroup emotional intelligence. Scale development and relationship to team process effectiveness and goal focus. *Human Resource Management Review, 12*, 195–214.

Jordan, P. J., & Troth, A. C. (2004). Managing emotions during team problem-solving: Emotional intelligence and conflict resolution. *Human Performance, 17*, 195–218.

Judge, T. A., Bono, J. E., Ilies, R., & Gerhardt, M. W. (2002). Personality and leadership: A qualitative and quantitative review. *Journal of Applied Psychology, 87*, 765–780.

Kaushal, R., & Kwanters, C. T. (2006). The role of culture and personality in choice of conflict management strategy. *International Journal of Intercultural Relations, 30*(5), 579–603.

Keegan, A., & Turner, J. R. (2001). Quantity versus quality in project-based learning practices. *Management Learning Journal, 32*(1), 77–98.

Keegan, A. E., & Hartog, D. N. (2004). Transformational leadership in a project-based environment: A comparative study of the leadership styles of project managers and line managers. *International Journal of Project Management, 22*(8), 609–618.

Keller, R. T. (2006). Transformational leadership, initiating structure, and substitutes for leadership: A longitudinal study of research and development project team performance. *Journal of Applied Psychology, 91*(1), 202–210.

Keltner, D., & Haidt, J. (2001). Social functions of emotion. In T. J. Mayne & G. A. Bonanno (Eds.), *Emotions: Current issues and future directions. Emotions and Social Behavior* (pp. 192–213). New York: Guilford.

Kerr, R., Garvin, J., Heaton, N., & Boyle, E. (2006). Emotional intelligence and leadership effectiveness. *Leadership & Organization Development Journal, 27*(4), 265–279.

Kerzner, H. (2001). *Project management: A systems approach to planning, scheduling and controlling.* New York: John Wiley.

Kim, S-I., & Rohner, R. P. (2003). Perceived parental acceptance and emotional empathy among university students in Korea. *Journal of Cross-Cultural Psychology, 34*(6), 723–735.

Kliem, R. L., & Ludin, I. S. (1992). *The people side of project management.* Aldershot: Gower.

Kloppenborg, T. J., & Petrick, J. A. (1999). Leadership in project life cycle and team character development. *Project Management Journal, 13*(2), 83–88.

Kolb, D. A. (1985). *Experiential Learning: Experience as the source of learning and development.* Englewood, NJ: Prentice-Hall.

Koman, E. S., & Wolff, S. B. (2008). Emotional intelligence competencies in the team and team leader. *Journal of Management Development, 27*(1), 55–75.

Kreiner, K. (1995). In search of relevance: Project management in drifting environments. *Scandinavian Journal of Management, 11*(4), 335–346.

Latham, G. P. (1988). Human resource training and development. *Annual Review of Psychology, 39*, 545–582.

Lave, J. & Wenger, E. (1991). *Situated learning: Legitimate peripheral participation.* Cambridge: Cambridge University Press.

Lazlo, Z., & Goldberg, A. I. (2008). Resource allocation uncertainty in a multi-project matrix environment: Is organizational conflict inevitable? *International Journal of Project Management, 26*(8), 773–788.

Leban, W., & Zulauf, C. (2004). Linking emotional intelligence abilities and leadership styles. *The Leadership and Organization Development Journal, 25*(7), 554–564.

Lechler, T. (1998). When it comes to project management, it's the people that matter: An empirical analysis of project management in Germany. In F. Hartman, G. Jergeas, & J. Thomas (Eds.), IRNOP III. *The nature and role of projects in the next 20 years: Research issues and problems.* (pp. 205–215). Calgary: University of Calgary.

Lee-Kelley, L., Leong, K., & Loong, K. (2003). Turner's five functions of project-based management and situational leadership in IT services projects. *International Journal of Project Management, 21*(8), 583–591.

Lester, D. L. (1998). Critical success factors for new product development. *Research Technology Management, 41*, Jan-Feb, 36–43.

Lewis, D. (1998). Competence-based management and corporate culture: Two theories with common flaws? *Long Range Planning, 31*(6), 937–943.

Lim, D. H., & Morris, M. L. (2006). Influence of trainee characteristics, instructional satisfaction and organizational climate on perceived training transfer. *Human Resource Development Quarterly, 17*(1), 85–115.

Locke, E. A. (2005). Why emotional intelligence is an invalid concept. *Journal of Occupational Behavior, 26*(4), 425–431.

Lopes, P. N., Brackett, M. A., Nezlek, J. B., Schutz, A., Sellin, I., & Salovey, P. (2004). Emotional intelligence and social interaction. *Personality & Social Psychology Bulletin, 30*(8), 1018–1034.

Lopes, P. N., Salovey, P., & Strauss, R. (2003). Emotional intelligence, personality and the perceived quality of social relationships. *Personality and Individual Differences, 35*, 641–658.

Lowe, K. B., Kroeck, K. G., & Sivasubramniam, N. (1996). Effectiveness correlates of transformational and transactional leadership: A meta-analytic review of the MLQ literature. *Leadership Quarterly, 7*(3), 385–425.

Lyle, J. (1997). *Understanding body language.* London: Chancellor Press.

Lynn, A. B. (2002). *The emotional intelligence activity book: 50 activities for promoting EQ at work.* New York: AMACOM Books.

Mabe, P., & West, S. (1982). Validity of self-evaluation of ability: A review and meta-analysis. *Journal of Applied Psychology, 67*, 280–296.

Maher, C. A. (1986). Evaluation of a program for improving conflict management skills of special service directors. *Journal of School Psychology, 24*(1), 45–53.

Makilouko, M. (2004). Coping with multicultural projects: The leadership styles of Finnish project managers. *International Journal of Project Management, 22*, 387–396.

Mandell, B., & Pherwani, S. (2003). Relationship between emotional intelligence and transformational leadership style: A gender comparison. *Journal of Business and Psychology, 17*(3), 387–404.

Marks, M. A., Mathieu, J. E., & Zaccaro, S. J. (2001). A temporally based framework and taxonomy of team processes. *Academy of Management Review, 26*(3), 356–376.

Marx, R. D. (1982). Relapse prevention for managerial training: A model for maintenance of behavior change. *Academy of Management Review, 7*(3), 433–441.

Matta, N. F., & Ashkenas, R. N. (2003). Why good projects fail anyway. *Harvard Business Review, 81*, September, 109–114.

Mayer, J. D., & Salovey, P. (1997). What is emotional intelligence? In P. Salovey & D. J. Sluyter (Eds.), *Educational development and emotional intelligence: Educational Implications.* New York: Basic Books.

Mayer, J. D., Salovey, P., & Caruso, D. R. (2002). *Mayer-Salovey-Caruso emotional intelligence test.* Toronto, Ontario: Multi Health Systems, Inc.

Mayer, J. D., Salovey, P., & Caruso, D. (2004). Emotional intelligence: Theory, findings and implications. *Psychological Inquiry, 15*, 97–105.

Mayer, J. D., Roberts, R. D., & Barsade, S. G. (2008). Human abilities: Emotional intelligence. *Annual Review of Psychology, 59*, 507–536

McAllister, D. J. (1995). Affect- and cognition-based trust as foundations for interpersonal co-operation in organizations. *Academy of Management Journal, 38*(1), 24–59.

McColl-Kennedy, J. R., & Anderson, R. D. (2002). Impact of leadership style on emotions on subordinate performance. *Leadership Quarterly, 13*, 545–59.

McCrae, R. R., & Costa, P. T., Jr. (1987). Validation of the five factor model of personality across instruments and observers. *Journal of Personality and Social Psychology, 52*, 81–90.

Megerian, L. E., & Sosik, J. J. (1996). An affair of the heart: Emotional intelligence and transformational leadership. *Journal of Leadership Studies, 3*, 31–48.

Mehrabian, A., & Epstein, N. (1972). A measure of emotional empathy. *Journal of Personality, 40*, 525–543.

Meyer, B. N., Fletcher, T. B., & Parker, S. J. (2004). Enhancing emotional intelligence in the health care environment: An exploratory study. *The Health Care Manager, 23* (3), 225–234.

Meyer, J. P., Stanley, D. J., Hersovitch, L., & Topolntsky, L. (2002). Affective, continuance and normative commitment to the organization: A meta-analysis of antecedents, correlates and consequences. *Journal of Vocational Behavior, 61*(1), 20–52.

Miles, M. B., & Huberman, M. A. (1994). *Qualitative data analysis: An expanded sourcebook.* London: Sage.

Milosevic, D., Inman, L., & Ozbay, A. (2001). Impact of project management standardization on project effectiveness. *Engineering Management Journal, 13*(4), 9–16.

Morand, D. A. (2001). The emotional intelligence of managers: Assessing the construct validity of a nonverbal measure of people skills. *Journal of Business and Psychology, 18*(1), 22–40.

Moriarty, P., & Buckley, F. (2003). Increasing team emotional intelligence through process. *Journal of European Industrial Training, 2* (2/3/4), 98–110.

Mount, J. (2006). The role of emotional intelligence in developing international business capability: EI provides traction. In V. U. Druskat, F. Sala, & J. Mount (Eds.), *Linking emotional intelligence and performance at work.* Mahwah, NJ: Lawrence Erlbaum Associates,

Muchinsky, P. (2000). Emotions in the workplace: The neglect of organizational behavior. *Journal of Organizational Behavior, 21*(7), 801–805.

Mueller, J., & Curham, J. (2006). Emotional intelligence and counterpart mood induction in a negotiation. *International Journal of Conflict Management, 17,* 110–28.

Muller, R., & Turner, J. R. (2007). Matching the project manager's leadership style to project type. *International Journal of Project Management, 25,* 21–32.

Mumford, M. (2003). Where have we been, where are we going? Taking stock in creativity research. *Creativity Research Journal, 15*(2&3), 107–120.

Mumford, M., & Licuanan, B. (2004). Leading for innovation: Conclusions, issues and directions. *The Leadership Quarterly, 15,* 163–171.

Mumford, M., Scott, G., Gaddis, B., & Strange, J. (2002). Leading creative people: Orchestrating expertise and relationships. *The Leadership Quarterly, 13,* 705–750.

Munns, A. K., & Bjeirmi, B. F. (1996). The role of project management in achieving project success. *International Journal of Project Management, 14*(2), 81–88.

Nemanich, L. A., & Vera, D. (2009). Transformational leadership and ambidexterity in the context of an acquisition. *The Leadership Quarterly, 20,* 19–33.

Nembhard, I. M., & Edmondson, A. C. (2006). Making it safe: The effects of leader inclusiveness and professional status on psychological safety and improvement efforts in health care teams. *Journal of Organizational Behavior, 27(7),* 941–966.

Newsome, S., Day, A. L., & Catano, V. M. (2000). Assessing the predictive validity of emotional intelligence. *Personality and Individual Differences, 29,* 1005–1016.

Nordin, F. (2006). Identity in intraorganisational and interorganisational alliance conflicts – a longitudinal study of an alliance pilot project in the high technology industry. *Industrial Marketing Management, 35*(2), 116–127.

Norrie, J., & Walker, D. H. T. (2004). A balanced scorecard approach to project management leadership, *Project Management Journal, 35*(4), 47–56.

Northouse, P. (2003). *Leadership: Theory and practice* (3rd ed.). London: Sage

Nunnally, J., & Bernstein, I. (1993). *Psychometric Theory* (3rd ed.). New York: McGraw-Hill.

O'Connor, M. M., & Reinsborough, L. (1992). Quality projects in the 1990s: A review of past projects and future trends. *International Journal of Project Management, 10*(2), 107–114.

O'Connor, R. M., & Little, I. S. (2003). Revisiting the predictive validity of emotional intelligence: Self-report versus ability-based measures. *Personality and Individual Differences, 35*, 1893–1902.

Offerman, L. R., Bailey, J. R., Vasilopoulos, N. L., Seal, C., & Sass, M. (2004). The relative contribution of emotional competence and cognitive ability to individual and team performance. *Human Performance, 17*(2), 219–243.

O'Leary, T., & Williams, T. (2008). Making a difference? Evaluating an innovative approach to the project management centre of excellence in a UK government department. *International Journal of Project Management, 26*, 556–565.

Olson, E. M., Walker, C. Jr., Rueckert, R. W., & Bonner, J. M. (2001). Patterns of cooperation during new product development among marketing, operations and R&D: Implications for project performance. *Journal of Product Innovation Management, 18*, 258–271.

Osborn, R. N., & Marion, R. (2009). Contextual leadership, transformational leadership and the performance of international innovation seeking alliances. *The Leadership Quarterly, 20*, 191–205.

Ozcelik, H., Langton, N., & Aldrich, H. (2008). Doing well and doing good: The relationship between leadership practices that facilitate a positive emotional climate and organizational performance. *Journal of Managerial Psychology, 23*(2), 186–203.

Pacala, J. T., Boult, C., Bland, C., & O'Brien, J. (1995). Aging game improves medical students caring for elders. *Gerontology and Geriatrics Education, 15*, 45–57.

Packendorff, J. (1995). Inquiring into the temporary organization: New directions for project management research. *Scandinavian Journal of Management, 11*(4), 319–333.

Palmer, B., Walls, M., Burgess, Z., & Stough, C. (2001). Emotional intelligence and effective leadership. *Leadership and Organization Development Journal, 22*, 1–7.

Pant, I., & Baroudi, B. (2008). Project management education: The human skills imperative. *International Journal of Project Management, 26*, 124–128.

Paulus, D. L., Lysy, D. C., & Yik, M. S. M. (1998). Self-report measures of intelligence: Are they useful as proxy IQ tests? *Journal of Personality, 66*, 525–553.

Pawar, B. S., & Eastman, K. K. (1997). The nature and implications of contextual influences on transformational leadership: A conceptual examination. *The Academy of Management Review, 22*, 80–109.

Peslak, A. R. (2005). Emotions and team projects and processes. *Team Performance Management, 11*(7/8), 251–262.

Petrides, K. V., & Furnham, A. (2003). Trait emotional intelligence: Behavioural validation in two studies of emotion recognition and reactivity to mood induction. *European Journal of Personality, 17*, 39–57.

Pinto, J. K. (2000). Understanding the role of politics in successful project management. *International Journal of Project Management, 18*(2), 85–91.

Pinto, J. K., & Slevin, D. P. (1988). Critical success factors across the project life cycle. *Project Management Journal, 19*(3), 67 –75.

Pinto, J. K., Thoms, P., Trailer, J., Palmer, T., & Govekar, M. (1998). *Project leadership from theory to practice.* Newtown Square, PA: Project Management Institute.

Phang, C. W., Kankanhalli, A., & Ang, C. (2008). Investigating organizational learning in eGovernment projects: A multi-theoretic approach. *Journal of Strategic Information Systems, 17*, 99–123.

Pirola-Merlo, A., Hartel, C., Mann, L., & Hirst, G. (2002). How leaders influence the impact of affective events on team climate and performance in R & D teams. *The Leadership Quarterly, 13*, 561–581.

Project Management Institute. (2007). *Project manager competency development framework* (2nd ed.). Newton Square, PA: Author.

PMI (2008). *A guide to the project management body of knowledge* (4th ed.), Newtown Square, PA: Project Management Institute.

Podsakoff, P. M., MacKenzie, S. B., Podsakoff, N. P., & Lee, Y. L. (2003). Common method biases in behavioral research: A critical review of the literature and recommended remedies. *Journal of Applied Psychology, 88*(5), 879–903.

Porter, L. W., & Lawler, E. E. (1968). *Managerial attitudes and performance.* Illinois: Irwin-Dorsey.

Porter, T. W., & Lilly, B. S. (1996). The effects of conflict, trust, and task commitment and project team performance. *International Journal of Conflict Management, 7*(4), 361–376.

Prabhakar, G. P. (2005). Switch leadership in projects: An empirical study reflecting the importance of transformational leadership on project success across twenty-eight nations. *Project Management Journal, 36*(4), 53–60.

Prati, L., Douglas, C., Ferris, G. R., Ammeter, A. P., & Buckley, M. R. (2003). Emotional intelligence, leadership effectiveness, and team outcomes. *International Journal of Organizational Analysis, 11*, 21–40.

Quinones, M. A., & Ehrenstein, A. (1997). Training for a rapidly changing workplace: Applications of psychological research. Washington, D.C: American Psychological Association.

Raelin, J. A. (2000) *Work-based learning: The new frontier of management development.* Upper Saddle River, NJ: Prentice-Hall.

Rahim, M. A., & Psenicka, C. (2002). A model of emotional intelligence and conflict management strategies: A study in seven countries. *The International Journal of Organizational Analysis, 10*(4), 302–326.

Randolph, W. A., & Posner, B. Z. (1988). What every manager needs to know about project management. *Sloan Management Review, Summer*, 65–73.

Rantanen, J., Metsapelto, R-L., Feldt, T., Pulkkinen, L., & Kokko, K. (2007). Long-term stability in the big-five personality traits in adulthood. *Scandinavian Journal of Psychology, 48*(6), 511–518.

Rapisarda, B. A. (2002). The impact of emotional intelligence on work team cohesiveness and performance. *International Journal of Organizational Analysis, 10*(4), 363–80.

Rickards, T., Chen, M-H., & Moger, S. (2001). Development of a self-report instrument for exploring team factor, leadership and performance relationships. *British Journal of Management, 12*, 243–250.

Riggio, R. E. (1986). Assessment of basic social skills. *Journal of Personality and Social Psychology, 51*, 649–660.

Riggio, R. E., & Reichard, R. J. (2008). The emotional and social intelligences of effective leadership: An emotional and social skill approach. *Journal of Managerial Psychology, 23*(2), 169–185.

Riggio, R. E., Riggio, H. R., Salinas, C., & Cole, E. J. (2003). The role of social and communication skills in leader emergence and effectiveness. *Group dynamics: Theory, research and practice, 7*(2), 83–103.

Roberts, R., Zeidner, M., & Matthews, G. M. (2001). Does emotional intelligence meet traditional standards for an intelligence? Some new data and conclusions. *Emotions, 1*, 196–231.

Rode, J. C., Mooney, C. H., Arthaud-Day, M. L., Near, J. P., Baldwin, T. L., Rubin, R. S., & Bommer, W. H. (2007). Emotional intelligence and individual performance: Evidence of direct and moderated effects. *Journal of Organizational Behavior, 28*, 399–421.

Roger, S., & Philip, L. (1997). Beyond the frame of management competenc(i)es: Towards a contextually embedded framework of managerial competence in organizations. *Journal of European Industrial Training, 21*(1), 26–33.

Rogers, C. R. (1975). Empathic: An unappreciated way of being. *Counseling Psychologist, 5*, 2–10.

Rosenthal, R. (1979). *Skill in nonverbal communication: Individual differences.* Cambridge, MA: Oelgeschlager, Gunn, & Hain.

Rosete, D., & Ciarrochi, J. (2005). Emotional intelligence and its relationship to workplace performance outcomes of leadership effectiveness. *Leadership and Organization Development Journal, 26*(5), 388–399.

Rouillier, J. Z., & Goldstein, I. L. (1993). The relationship between organizational transfer climate and positive transfer of training. *Human Resource Development Quarterly, 4*(4), 377–390.

Rudolph, T., Wagner, T., & Fawcett, S. (2008). Project management in retailing: Integrating the behavioral dimension. *The International Review of Retail, Distribution and Consumer Research, 18*(3), 325–341

Ruuska, I., & Vartiainen, M. (2003). Critical project competences—A case study. *Journal of Workplace Learning, 15*(7/8), 307–312.

Sala, F. (2006). *Do programs designed to increase emotional intelligence at work – work?* Available at www.eiconsortium.org/research/do_ei_programs_work .htm.

Salancik, G. R., & Pfeffer, J. (1978). A social information processing approach to job attitudes and task design. *Administrative Science Quarterly, 23,* 224–253.

Salas, E., Sims, D. E., & Burke, C. S. (2005). Is there a big five in teamwork? *Small Group Research, 36*(5), 555–599.

Salovey, P., & Mayer, J. D. (1990). Emotional intelligence. *Imagination, Cognition & Personality, 9,* 185–211.

Schmidt, F. L. & Hunter, J. E. (1998). The validity and utility of selection methods in personnel psychology: Practical and theoretical implications of 85 years of research findings. *Psychological Bulletin, 124,* 262–274.

Schutte, N. S., Malouff, J. M., Hall, L. E., Haggerty, D. J., Cooper, J. T., Golden, C.J., & Dornheim, L. (1998). Development and validation of a measure of emotional intelligence. *Personality & Individual Differences, 25,* 167–177.

Sense, A. J. (2003). A model of the politics of project leader learning. *International Journal of Project Management, 21,* 107–114.

Shapiro, J. A., Morrison, E. H., & Boker, J. R. (2004). Teaching empathy to first year medical students: Evaluation of an elective literature and medicine course. *Education for Health, 17*(1), 73–84.

Sicotte, H., & Langley, A. (2000). Integration mechanisms and R&D project performance. *Journal of Engineering and Technology Management, 17,* 1–37.

Sivanathan, N., & Fekken, G. (2002). Emotional intelligence, moral reasoning and transformational leadership. *Leadership & Organization Development Journal, 23*(4), 198–204.

Sizemore House, R. (1988). The human side of project management. Reading, MA: Addison-Wesley.

Skinner, C., & Spurgeon, P. (2005). Valuing empathy and emotional intelligence in health leadership: A study of empathy, leadership behaviour and outcome effectiveness. *Health Services Management Research, 18,* 1–12.

Slaski, M., & Cartwright, S. (2003). Emotional intelligence training and its implications for stress, health and performance. *Stress and Health, 19*(4), 233–239.

Slevin, D. P., & Pinto, J. K. (1991). Project leadership: Understanding and consciously choosing your style. *Project Management Journal, 22*(1), 29–47.

Sommerville, J., & Langford, V. (1994). Multivariate influences on the people side of projects: Stress and conflict. *International Journal of Project Management, 12*(4), 234–243.

Sosik, J. J., & Megerian, J. (1999). Understanding leader emotional intelligence and performance. *Group and Organization Management, 24,* 367–391.

Spearman, C. (1927). *The abilities of man.* New York: Macmillan.

Spector, P. E. (1987). Method variance as an artifact in self-reported affect and perceptions at work: Myth or significant problem. *Journal of Applied Psychology, 72,* 438–443.

Spector, P. E. (1994). Using self-report questionnaires in OB research: A comment on the use of a controversial method. *Journal of Organizational Behavior, 15,* 385–392.

Staw, B. M., & Barsade, S. G. (1993). Affect and managerial performance: A test of the sadder-but-wise vs. happier-and-smarter hypothesis. *Administrative Science Quarterly, 38*, 304–331.

Steiner, I. D. (1972). *Group processes and productivity.* New York: Academic Press.

Stogdill, R. M. (1974). *Handbook of leadership: Survey of the literature.* New York: Free Press.

Strang, K. D. (2005). Examining effective and ineffective transformational project leadership. *Team Performance Management, 11*(3/4), 68–103.

Strohmeier, S. (1992). Development of interpersonal skills for senior project managers. *International Journal of Project Management, 10*(1), 45–48.

Sunindijo, R. Y., Hadikusumo, B. H. W., & Ogunlana, S. (2007). Emotional intelligence and leadership styles in construction project management. *Journal of Management in Engineering, 23*(4), 166–170.

Sweeney, P. J., & Lee, D. R. (1999). Support and commitment factors of project teams. *Engineering Management Journal, 11*(3), 13–18.

Sy, T., Cote, S., & Saavedra, R. (2005). The contagious leader: Impact of the leader's mood on the mood of group members, group affective tone, and group processes. *Journal of Applied Psychology, 90*(2), 295–305.

Taborda, C. G. (2000). Leadership, teamwork and empowerment: Future management trends. *Cost Engineering, 42*(10), 41–44.

Tannenbaum, S. J., Mathieu, J. E., Salas, E., & Canon-Bowers, J. A. (1991). Meeting trainees' expectations: The influence of training fulfillment on the development of commitment, self efficacy and motivation. *Journal of Applied Psychology, 76*(6), 759–769.

Tarr, P. (2007). Epupa Dam Case Study. *Water Resources Development, 23*(3), 473–484.

Terje, I. V. (2004). Improving project collaboration: Start with the conflicts. *International Journal of Project Management, 22*(6), 447–454.

Terje, I. V., & Hakansson, H. (2003). Exploring interorganizational conflict in complex projects. *Industrial Marketing Management, 32*(2), 127–138.

Thambain, H. J. (2004). Team leadership effectiveness in technology-based project environments. *Project Management Journal, 35*(4), 35–46.

Thirty, M. (2004). How can the benefits of PM training programs be improved. *International Journal of Project Management, 22*(1), 13–18.

Thurstone, L. L. (1938). Primary mental abilities. *Psychological Monographs,* No.1.

Thorndike, E. L. (1920). Intelligence and its uses. *Harper Magazine, 140*, 227–235.

Tisher, A., Dvir, D., Shenhar, A., & Lipovetsky, S. (1996). Identifying critical success factors in defense development projects: A multivariate analysis. *Technological Forecasting and Social Change, 51*(2), 151–171.

Tracey, J. B., Tannenbaum, S. I., & Kavagnah, M. J. (1995). Applying trained skills on the job: The importance of the work environment. *Journal of Applied Psychology, 80*, 239–252.

Turner, J. & Keegan, A. (1999). The management of operations in the project-based organization. In K. A. Artto, K. Kahkonen, & K. Koskinen (Eds.), *Managing business by projects,* Vol 1. Project Management Association, Finland and NORDNET, Helsinki, 57–85.

Turner, R., & Lloyd-Walker, B. (2008). Emotional intelligence (EI) Capabilities training: Can it develop EI in project teams?

Turner, R. J. (1999). *The handbook of project-based management: Improving the process for achieving strategic objectives.* New York: McGraw-Hill.

Turner, R. J., & Muller, R. (2005). The project manager's leadership style as a success factor on projects: A literature review. *Project Management Journal,* 36(2), 49–61.

Verma, V. K. (1996). *Human resource skills for the project manager,* Vol 2. Newtown Square, PA: Project Management Institute.

Waldman, D. A., & Yammarino, F. J. (1999). CEO charismatic leadership: Levels of management and levels of analysis effects. *Academy of Management Review, 24,* 266–285.

Watkin, C. (2000). Developing emotional intelligence. *International Journal of Selection and Assessment, 8*(2), 89–92.

Webb, A. (2000). *Project management for successful product innovation.* Basingstoke: Gower.

Webster-Stratton, C., & Hammond, M. (1999). Marital conflict management skills, parenting style and early onset conduct problems: Processes and pathways. *Journal of Child Psychology and Psychiatry, 40*(6), 917–927.

Wechsler, D. (1958). *The measurement and appraisal of adult intelligence* (4th ed.). Baltimore, MD: Williams and Wilkins.

Weick, K. E., & Roberts, K. H. (1993). Collective mind in organizations: Heedful interrelating on flight decks. *Administrative Science Quarterly, 38,* 356–381.

Weiss, H. M., & Cropanzano, R. (1996). Affective events theory: A theoretical discussion of the structure, causes, and consequences of affective experiences at work. *Research in Organizational Behavior, 18,* 1–74.

Wexley, K. N., & Baldwin, T. T. (1986). Posttraining strategies for facilitating positive transfer: An empirical exploration. *Academy of Management Review, 29*(3), 503–520.

Williams, T. (1999). The need for new paradigms for complex projects. *International Journal of Project Management, 17*(5), 269–273.

Williams, T. (2005). Assessing and building on project management theory in the light of badly over-run projects. *IEEE Trans-Engineering Management, 52*(4), 497–508.

Winter, M., & Thomas, J. (2004). Understanding the lived experience of managing projects: The need for more emphasis on the practice of managing. In D. P. Slevin, D. I. Cleland, & J. K. Pinto (Eds.), *Innovations: Project management research 2004,* (pp. 419–438). Newtown Square, PA: Project Management Institute.

Winter, M., Smith, C., Morris, P., & Cicmil, S. (2006). Directions for future research in project management: The main findings of a UK government funded research network. *International Journal of Project Management, 24,* 638–649.

Wolff, S. B., Pescosolido, A. T., & Druskat, V. (2002). Emotional intelligence as the basis of leadership emergence in self-managing teams. *The Leadership Quarterly, 13*, 505–522.

Wonderlic & Associates (1983). *Wonderlic Personnel Test Manual.* Northfield, IL: Wonderlic, Inc.

Wong, C. S., Foo, M. D., Wang, C. W., & Wong, P. M. (2007). The feasibility of training and development of EI: An exploratory study in Singapore, Hong Kong and Taiwan. *Intelligence, 35*(92), 141–150.

Yammarino, F. J., Spangler, W. D., & Bass, R. M. (1993). Transformational leadership and performance: A longitudinal investigation. *Leadership Quarterly, 4*(1), 81–102.

Yukl, G. (1998). *Leadership in organizations* (4th ed.). Englewood Cliffs, NJ: Prentice Hall.

Zeidner, M., Matthews, G., & Roberts, R. D. (2004). Emotional intelligence in the workplace: A critical review. *Applied psychology: An international review, 53*(3), 371–399.

Zhou, J., & George, M. (2001). Awakening employee creativity: The role of leader emotional intelligence. *The Leadership Quarterly, 14*, 545–568.

Zimmerer, T. W., & Yasin, M. M. (1998). A leadership profile of American Project Managers. *Project Management Journal, 21*(1), 31–38.